BEYOND THE BURNING BUS

BEYOND THE BURNING BUS

The Civil Rights Revolution
in a Southern Town

PHIL NOBLE

FOREWORD BY WILLIAM B. MCCLAIN
INTRODUCTION BY NAN WOODRUFF

NewSouth Books
Montgomery

NewSouth Books
P.O. Box 1588
Montgomery, AL 36102

Library of Congress Cataloging-in-Publication Data
Noble, Phil.
Beyond the burning bus : the civil rights revolution in a southern
town / Phil Noble ; foreword by Bob McClain ; introduction by Nan
Woodruff.
p. cm.
Includes bibliographical references and index.
ISBN 1-58838-120-X
1. African Americans—Civil rights—Alabama—Anniston—History—
20th century. 2. Anniston (Ala.)—Race relations. 3.Violence—
Alabama—Anniston—History—20th century. 4. Civil rights
workers—Crimes against—Alabama—Anniston—History—20th
century. 5.Crimes aboard buses—Alabama—Anniston—History—
20th century. 6. Congress of Racial Equality—History. 7. Civil rights
movements—Southern States—History—20th century. I. Title.
F334.A6N63 2003
976.1'63—dc21
2003007411

Design by Randall Williams
Printed in the United States of America

TO

POPESY, BETTY, PHIL, AND SCOTT,

WHO LIVED THIS STORY WITH ME.

A MORE WONDERFUL FAMILY THAN

I COULD EVER HAVE DREAMED OF,

AND A SPECIAL GIFT FROM GOD.

Contents

Foreword

BY WILLIAM B. McCLAIN

WHEN I FINISHED Boston University School of Theology in 1962, I headed straight back to northeast Alabama, where I was born and raised, to be a pastor. The church to which I had been appointed in June had patiently and perhaps somewhat anxiously waited for their new young pastor to finish his early degree in summer school, get married, go on a honeymoon, and arrive in time to preach and celebrate communion on the first Sunday in September. I was now the twenty-four-year-old pastor of Haven Chapel Methodist Church in Anniston, the largest Negro Methodist Church in Calhoun County, with a membership of four hundred and eleven, a very good-sized church in any city, and especially in that part of Alabama in those days.

Haven Chapel was a proud historic church dating back to the last of the nineteenth century. It was middle-class in its mentality, if not altogether in its makeup. It boasted of having most of Anniston's educated black citizens—primarily classroom teachers, principals and coaches, and a few others who had attended college but worked at mainly menial jobs or in factories. Anniston then had one black dentist, two black medical doctors (one was retired and the father of the dentist), and no lawyers of color. None of these medical persons, by the way, were members of the Baptist or Methodist churches. Little did the people of Haven Chapel note that many of our people were maids across town, janitors in various white establishments, factory and furnace workers, and laborers and workers at that deadly Monsanto Plant that I can still smell after forty years.

Most of the rest of the so-called "middle-class Negroes of Anniston" were members of Seventeenth Street Baptist Church, a church with the same basic profile as Haven Chapel. Its pastor was and still is the Rev. Dr. Nimrod Q. Reynolds, a man of great courage, intellect, conviction, passion for justice, and a pastor extraordinaire. I still marvel at his organizational skills, his tender heart for people, and his dogged determination. He became my closest associate in the struggle for civil rights. He remains, at this writing, one of my dearest friends. The only real difference between our churches was that one was Baptist, and proud to be so; the other was Methodist, and equally proud to be so. Otherwise, their members were just Negro citizens of Anniston who were racially segregated just like all the people of their color in this town.

In Anniston, as in Atlanta, Savannah, Charleston, Charlotte and throughout the beautiful South of my love and my birth, all was segregated: buses, bus and train terminals, churches, restrooms, schools, hospitals, neighborhoods, lunch counters, everything. There were bold "white" and "colored" signs on public water fountains and restrooms, separate entrances to public places, and an understanding of race and place deeply and carefully embedded in the psyche of both races. By this conventional interpretation of race and reality all were expected to live. Or die. And the cemeteries were segregated, too!

Even though I had been born in Gadsden, just thirty miles north of Anniston and just as segregated—if not more so, because of it being about twice the size of Anniston—I did not, and could not, and refused to allow myself to accept the interpretation that I was inferior and those human arrangements were either final or creditable. The governors of Alabama and Mississippi and Georgia had declared in no uncertain terms that segregation would be forever. Their steadfast stances were covered by the media with regularity and fanfare. This only served to make racial

_____

THE REV. DR. WILLIAM B. "BOB" MCCLAIN *is a native of Gadsden, Alabama, whose first pastorate was Anniston's Haven Chapel Methodist Church. Today he is the Mary Elizabeth Joyce Professor of Preaching and Worship at Wesley Theological Seminary, Washington, D.C. His undergraduate degree is from Clark College and his master's and doctoral degrees are from Boston University. He is the author of many articles and eight books.*

encounters more cruel and generously misendowed with a legacy of hatred and denigration endemic to the culture. But I was a Christian and a minister and what I saw with my eyes did not square with what I knew the Gospel of Jesus Christ to declare and mean. Armed with my own recent experiences of Boston and New York, a mission work camp in the Kokee mountains of Hawaii, and travel to other places where I had seen a different racial scenario—although far from perfect—I was determined to challenge this way of living in Anniston and anywhere else I was segregated and treated as inferior. I was determined to spend the rest of my life, if necessary, working, preaching, teaching, marching, writing, being arrested, and doing whatever else I could do or had to do to change this racial arrangement. I would accept this inferior role and this dehumanizing segregated system no longer! No matter what it took! If that meant dying, I was prepared to die! I had had enough, and my soul knew that quite well! My whole being, every fiber of it, knew: "No more segregation and injustice for me! I am prepared to die to change it."

I was also clear about something else (and I still am): not all white people were bad, and not all white people believed that this racial arrangement was right—even those who lived in Anniston in 1962. Some of those people who lived in Anniston had been "up North," had vacationed in Europe, Asia, and other foreign countries. They had seen all kinds of people mingle and live together without regard to skin color.

President Truman had already desegregated the military, in spite of the protests of Strom Thurman and the "Dixiecrats." Many white military veterans living in Anniston had been to countries like Italy and Belgium, England, and Sweden. Surely, I knew, there had to be some persons in Anniston who had seen life lived differently, and who had guts enough to stand up and say so! Surely there must be some people who knew that segregation and discrimination are evil. Surely there must be some educated white Christians who knew theology and ethics and that racism is sin. After all, this was after World War II, where even the savagery of Aryanism and Naziism, and the wholesale destruction of the Jews, had not razed all of the synagogues, temples, and cathedrals. There must be some decency left in the human breast. Surely not everyone was willing to capitulate to this heinous evil. Where were the white people like the white professors I had known in Atlanta, Georgia, in a small Negro Methodist college? Where were those selfless white women who had forfeited fame, fortune and family to plant the freeing touch of literacy and education in the Southern stygian dark skies after the so-called emancipation?

The question was: who were those white people in Anniston? How did you find them in such a segregated arrangement? And what would you do when you did find them? I knew that there would be no social integration, no acceptance of persons as persons, of equals looking across the table at each other, or better still, "breaking bread together as equally sinful and forgiven," but what about *de jure?* At least, for now!

One thing quickly became clear as I started this quest: my partners and allies and crusaders would not be the Methodist pastors. They would not lead the way to changing Anniston or anything else that had to do with "putting yourself on the line." Dan Whitsett, a Methodist preacher in Sylacauga, just a few miles away, had already been "shipped out by night" for taking a stand on these matters. I had known him when I was in high school and president of the Annual Conference Methodist Youth Fellowship in the segregated Central Jurisdiction of the Methodist Church. I had met him again when I was a seminary student at Boston University. He was then in Cambridge, Massachusetts, where he had to go to make his stand on race and had become the pastor of a church near Harvard University. Not one of Anniston's white Methodist pastors whom I called on the telephone was willing to meet me in person—at their place or mine! I thought, how could we be in the same church, meet in New York or Chicago at a national meeting of the same church and come back to Alabama and be so separated, so isolated, so overwhelmingly different? But it was so! It was amazingly so in the Anniston, Alabama, to which I was appointed in 1962 to live and to serve as pastor.

But Rev. Nimrod Q. Reynolds and I teamed up to fight segregation in Anniston. It was clear to me when I first met him that we were kindred spirits. It was not just that we had both gone to Clark College (though we had not been there at the same time and we were members of different denominations and different fraternities). But the more we talked about the plight of black people, the more we knew we were a team and had to do something. And we began to search for some brave white soul who would at least talk to us about "the problem," that problem W. E. B. DuBois had identified as the major one for America for the twentieth century—the "color line." That person turned out to be not a Methodist like me or a Baptist like Rev. Reynolds, but a Presbyterian minister, J. Phillips Noble, the pastor of the First Presbyterian Church of Anniston, this book, who attempts in this book to recall and relate the days and details of our struggle to change the racial arrangements and the racial xenophobic atmosphere of Anniston, Alabama.

I remember well our initial meeting in his church office as Rev. Reynolds and I cautiously and fearfully but determinedly made our way across town. We were on a mission and we were not sure how it would turn out, but we both knew that we had to go. I think I could say about that meeting and the subsequent events and actions that are chronicled in this book by Phil Noble, what Peter Storey has written about his involvement in South Africa and the efforts to end apartheid there. Storey is a white South African Methodist clergyman, now teaching at Duke University Divinity School in Durham, North Carolina. He is a veteran of the war against apartheid where he was one of the few white clergymen to stand with the black South Africans and to lead protests against that heinous system of racial segregation and xenophobia in that part of the world. About that experience and his prophetic vocation, he wrote: "The miracle South African Christians have to proclaim is not the story of their faithfulness; it is the wonder of a God who could use such a feeble witness so powerfully. And the question must arise, 'What if the witness had been stronger? What could God not do with a truly faithful Church, willing to take on the world?'" [Peter Storey, *With God in the Crucible* (Nashville: Abingdon Press, 2002), p. 17].

Looking back across the span of forty years, I wonder what could have happened if the "witness had been stronger" in Anniston, Alabama, if all those who professed Christianity and who led the Christian churches had marched out shoulder to shoulder against our Southern apartheid. But, the times were what they were, and on that day, Rev. Reynolds and I felt as we crossed over to the other side of town to meet with the Rev. Phillips Noble of the white First Presbyterian Church, that we were "taking on the world." Our question was, "Will we find this white minister faithful and willing to join us?" "Is he going to be the one?" After we laid before this white minister the racial situation, our feelings, the evils of segregation, discrimination, injustice, economic and political deprivation, the right to vote, the suffering and plight of our people, and the concomitant requirements of the Gospel to right the wrongs and our perceived role, we detected some sympathy and even a sense of identification. It was there and we knew it. That was confirmed as Phil Noble, a white Presbyterian minister, joined hands with a black Methodist minister and a black Baptist minister in a circle of prayer. He suggested prayer and we prayed. By the time Phil's prayer was over, we were all in tears. We had not only joined hands, we had joined our hearts in an effort that we saw as more than a civil rights campaign for social and economic change, more than simply an effort to peacefully desegregate Anniston, more than a social movement, but one that involved our deepest spiritual commitment and calling. We have remained colleagues and close and respected friends ever since. It was a friendship and a collegiality forged in the crucible. It then and now calls us to a life of costly discipleship.

We could not wait to get back across town to tell our mutual colleague and older friend, the late George Smitherman, the pastor of the largest Baptist church in town, Mt. Calvary, of our experience with the Rev. Phillips Noble, the pastor of First Presbyterian Church. When we blurted it out with our black preacher excitement, he was incredulous! The proof had to be provided.

That proof is what Phil Noble writes about in this book: the meetings of the clergy, the behind-the-scenes conversations and strategies, the forming of the Bi-Racial Council, the civil rights campaign, the changes made, and so on. But Phil Noble also writes in this book about his own struggle and conviction about race and religion, his own struggle to be faithful to what he believed and felt. None of this we knew before we made the trip across town.

Etched indelibly in my memory is that awful Sunday when Rev. Reynolds and I were assaulted, shot at, beaten by the huge white mob of the Ku Klux Klan and the White Citizens' Council in front of the Carnegie Public Library in Anniston. It is still referred to by white people in Anniston and the *Anniston Star* as "The Incident at the Library." That is not the way black people remember it, and certainly not the way Rev. Reynolds and I recall it. I know that the bullet fired at close range into Rev. Reynolds's car only narrowly missed the nape of my neck—coming to lodge in the edge of the back of the front driver's side seat. We both know that that was the day when death waited, yet our lives were spared!

We were simply attempting to "integrate" the public library by checking out a book as we had pre-agreed with Anniston's Human Relations Council to do. Where did the mob come from? Why did they know about the arrangements to which Rev. Reynolds and I were sworn to secrecy? We did not even tell our wives where we were going. How did that many obvious "thugs" gather at a downtown library on a Sunday afternoon without being noticed? In those days "decent people" dressed up on Sunday in the South. Why weren't we warned about their presence? Where were the police who guard and patrol the city streets? These are just some of the questions that remain in our minds. Some of the answers to questions we still have about "The Incident" died with the people who knew. Some of the answers still lie with those who are living yet and who never told the whole truth! But our lives were spared to continue the fight. We have both continued to preach an uncompromising gospel of love, power and justice for all God's children. We have both remained activists and engaged in the struggle for justice and liberation as a major part of our ministries. The so-called "Incident" happened on the very same Sunday that four little black girls lost their lives in Birmingham, Alabama, at the Sixteenth Street Baptist Church when the church was bombed by a similar group of people, or maybe the same ones, for all we know.

I regret that "Old Brother George Smitherman," the wisest among us, did not live to be able to read this account Phil Noble has written about those days in Anniston that now seem so long ago. He would have been one of the persons I would have turned to and asked to reflect on those days. But he took eternal residence a while ago in a "beautiful City" beyond the Jasmine walls. If he were still here, I am sure he would offer his corrections and his folksy and wise comments on what really happened in Anniston, Alabama, from the perspective of the black community.

Phil Noble is to be commended for staying at the task and helping all of us to remember what it took to move a sleepy, Southern city a little bit forward toward racial integration and equality. He was a faithful witness and a vital part of Anniston coming to grips with its myriad racial problems. In telling the story of Anniston and the sixties, he is in the center for change and progress. Phil Noble was key to getting any "movement," so to speak, in Anniston. His role was crucial also in avoiding any more bloodshed than there was. I always make that crystal clear as I tell the story of racial change in Anniston, Alabama—whether to primarily black audiences or white. I still marvel at his courage, his willingness to speak the truth to Caesar, and to be a bridge person as he rightly tells in this story. I also marvel at what we were able to accomplish with as little bloodshed in some difficult and dangerous days. God knows it could have been worse, and came very close to it on that Sunday night, September 15, 1963, when there were more on the outside of a packed 17th Street Church than there were on the inside. They were prepared to defend their leaders, assault the city, and to avenge the dignity, honor and person of their pastors and their leaders. Thank God they heard and heeded the message of non-violence piped by loudspeaker from the inside to the outside.

There were forces for segregation that were dangerously alive—not only in the secular Anniston, but also in the churches, including Phil's church. There were cauldrons of searing heat and hate all around. And there were those who vehemently opposed his involvement and his stance. So his was a bit more than a feeble effort. In fact, the collective effort of all of us in Anniston who worked for peaceful change was a commendable and courageous struggle against powerful and wide-ranging forces for evil and America's brand of apartheid.

Preface

THE U.S. SUPREME COURT's *Brown* v. *Board of Education* decision made 1954 a watershed year. For the next quarter-century, the nation struggled with the long-overdue changes that resulted from the implementation of that decision and its ripple effect on laws and racial mores. Indeed, many historians and participants in the events that profoundly reshaped American society would argue that the struggle is far from over today. What is indisputable is that the *Brown* decision triggered a civil rights revolution. The revolution was fought in places large and small. Some of its battles became well-known and the men and women involved in them became famous or infamous. Other battles, more numerous, are remembered today mostly in the places where they occurred and by the people who took part in them. Collectively, these well-known and unknown battles made up the modern Civil Rights Movement.

This small book tells the story of how the national and even international movement toward racial justice played itself out in one medium-sized church in one medium-sized city in the Deep South.

Early on there were two small symbols for me of the struggle to come, a struggle that would bring deep tension and at times grave danger. The first symbol was in June 1954 when I was a commissioner to the General Assembly of the Presbyterian Church, U.S., meeting in Richmond, Virginia. The Supreme Court's *Brown* decision had been announced the previous month, and the Assembly took an action indicating its approval. In the morning worship service on the Sunday after I returned to Greenville, South Carolina, where I was the minister at the Second Presbyterian Church, I stated that I was proud of the Presbyterian Church for its stand. A deacon immediately stood up in the congregation, walked down the aisle and out the back door, which he slammed.

The noise that reverberated throughout the sanctuary was a portent of things to come. Before the next fifteen years would be over, there would be conflict—sometimes violent—in which doors would be slammed shut, pried open, and broken down.

A door seems such a simple thing, but mighty controversy can swirl around whether a door should be open or shut, who opens or shuts it, who can go through it and who cannot, and when it should be open and when shut. White church people debated heatedly whether their church doors should be open or closed to blacks. Governor George Wallace stood in a doorway in a symbolic attempt to keep a black student from enrolling in the University of Alabama. Other Southern governors and officials vowed to do all in their power to keep blacks from entering public institutions or using public facilities that had for decades been preserved for the use of whites. These segregationists and "defenders of the Southern way of life" received wide support throughout the white community. Many of the officials and their supporters were members of Christian churches.

The second symbol was given to me in 1956, when I became the minister of the First Presbyterian Church of Anniston, Alabama. After being there a few months, I went down to register to vote. I entered the courthouse and went into the designated room where a woman at a desk gave me forms to fill out and sign. Three or four black people were also in the room working on their forms. I observed as one of the black women went to the desk to ask a question. What caught my attention was the harsh, rude manner in which the black woman was told that she could not be given any help, and that if she could not fill out the form, she could not be registered to vote. Suspecting that the clerk's demeanor was intended to discourage blacks from voting, I decided to ask a question, which was answered politely.

I completed the form and the clerk was noticeably polite as I handed it to her. She quickly scanned the form. One question had asked: "Will you support the government of the United States of America and the State of Alabama?" In answer I had written, "Yes, in that order." I hadn't intended to raise any controversy although I was very much aware that the *Brown* decision had resulted in renewed widespread questioning by segregationists of the Federal government's authority versus that of the states—in other words, state's rights. Perhaps this awareness had been subconsciously pricked by the rude treatment of the black woman.

In any case, the clerk asked, "What do you mean by that answer?" I politely said (after all, I was the new minister), "The question asks if I will support the government of the United States and that of Alabama, and I answered that I would in the order the governments were indicated in the question, that is, the United States first and then Alabama." She replied, "Well, that is what the question says, so will you be willing just to answer 'Yes'?" I replied, "If that is what the question means, then my answer has not said anything different." She repeated with some agitation, "Is it all right to change the answer to simply 'Yes'?"

I reflected a moment, sensing something of the larger tension relating to black people's right to vote, and said, "No, I believe I would like to leave the answer as I've written it." She replied, "Then I cannot register you to vote. I will have to take it up with the Commission."

Later, I did receive notice indicating that the Commission had registered me as a voter, but not before one of the elders in my church laughingly told me that a member of the Commission who was a friend of his had asked him if their new minister was "a Communist." He had replied that so far as he knew I was not! This would not be the last time I would be suspected of being a Communist.

This very small incident was a clear symbol of the struggle that was to come. Voting rights, the openness of churches, institutions, and public facilities, and countless spin-off issues occupied a large part of my thought, energy and work for the next fifteen years.

The story told here is unique in one sense. However, in a larger sense this is the story of the grassroots civil rights revolution as it occurred in many communities. In some areas the white Christian church has been vilified for not taking a stand for civil rights, and for not doing more for the cause of freedom and justice in our society. I wanted to tell this story to show what some white ministers and churches in the white community did. While it is true that some ministers and churches did little or nothing, or worse, were a part of the segregationist resistance to civil rights, there were many that quietly did a great deal.

This is a story that happened forty years ago. Many people, born in the decades since then have little knowledge of the events of the 1960s. In May 16, 2000, the last two suspects in the bombing of the Sixteenth Baptist Church in Birmingham were indicted by an Alabama grand jury for murder and subsequently convicted. The defendants had walked free from prosecution for almost forty years. When my daughter, Dr. Betty Scott Noble, walked into her office, having heard on her car radio the news of the grand jury indictments, she said to her administrative assistant, "I am glad that after all these years following the Birmingham Church bombing, that the authorities have arrested and charged with murder, those who did the bombing." Her assistant was a very intelligent young woman who had graduated from Agnes Scott College and was working on a master's degree. She replied, "I don't know what you are talking about." Amazed, Betty said, "You don't know about the bombing of the Sixteenth Street Baptist Church in Birmingham in the 1960s when four little black girls were killed?" Her assistant said, "No, I never knew anything about it." This illustrates what may be the situation with numerous young people of this generation.

I think that young people, black and white, need to know the meaning of the struggle of the 1960s, with its dangers and the sacrifices that were made, and to appreciate the results, which they enjoy today in terms of freedom and justice. Also, I know there are still many of my generation who have not correctly interpreted the meaning and significance of the events of the decade of the sixties.

My involvement in the Civil Rights Revolution in Anniston had a genuine effect on my children. They are now grown and it pleases me that I can see no racial prejudice in their attitudes. It is also good to observe that my two grandchildren, JP and Lizzie, are being brought up by Phil Jr. and Nancy to have no racial prejudice. If the telling of this story can help create a similar effect on others, then I will be gratified.

Acknowledgments

T HIS BOOK would never have been written but for the insistence of my family. They lived through this story with me, and they thought it needed to be told. With all deliberate haste I got around to it almost forty years later! Part of my reluctance was because many had lost their lives in the Civil Rights struggle, and others had suffered from physical and emotional violence and other hardships, and I had not really suffered. I lived through dangers and times of real anxiety, but nothing like what so many others experienced.

Three Ph.D.'s read my manuscript and "culled out my Mississippi grammar." My daughter Betty Scott Noble, a psychologist with a private practice in Atlanta, who also teaches at Agnes Scott College, first went through the manuscript with a fine toothcomb. Martha Hay Vardeman, a sociologist who taught at Stillman College in Tuscaloosa, Alabama, for sixteen years and at Oglethorpe University in Atlanta for twenty-three years, made corrections. This was followed by the comments and suggestions and corrections by Nan Woodruff, professor of Southern History at Penn State University. I am also grateful to her for writing the Introduction.

Morris Dees of the Southern Poverty Law Center, to whom I am grateful, read my manuscript and sent it to Randall Williams, editor of Newsouth Books. Randall and his partner Suzanne La Rosa accepted the book for publication, and I owe much to Randall for his editing skills, by which the manuscript has been much improved. It has been a pleasure to work with the good NewSouth Books team: Suzanne La Rosa, Randall Williams, Mildred Wakefield, Foster Dickson, Amanda Davis, Rhonda Reynolds, and Patrick Steele.

Others who are part of the story made major contributions. Miller and Barbara Sproull read the manuscript, made suggestions, and helped gather many of the pictures that are included. Dr. William B. McClain, professor of preaching at Wesley Seminary in Washington, D.C., was a strong supporter of my writing the story, and has written the Foreword. Dr. Nimrod Q. Reynolds urged me onward, gathered pictures, and gave me his encouragement. Interviews with Ellis R. Grier, Edward Wood, E. C. Talbert, and the Rev. Judge L. Stringer were most helpful in giving me a better understanding of some of the things that were happening in the black community. Claude Dear, who was mayor of Anniston when the events of the story occurred, was most generous and helpful in sharing his scrapbook of this period and his recollections of events. Charlie Doster was most helpful in providing some details. Brandt Ayers, publisher of the *Anniston Star*, and his executive secretary, Sherry Kughn, were helpful with their advice, as was Jeannie Thompson, executive director of the Alabama Writers Forum. Patsy Wilkinson typed the first very rough draft of the manuscript. Others too numerous to name have helped in various ways and have my appreciation.

My son, Phil Noble, Jr., may have given me the best advice and encouragement of all as he kept saying, "Write it. Just write it." Finally, it would be hard to imagine a more supportive wife than Betty Pope Scott Noble, known from childhood as "Popesy," who not only encouraged me in the writing of this story, but who was a constant and enthusiastic companion in fifty years of ministry. Without her the half would not have been done.

Introduction

By Nan Woodruff

When anyone familiar with the civil rights movement thinks of Anniston, Alabama, images immediately come to mind of a blazing Greyhound bus with smoke spiraling from its windows, of passengers scrambling to escape, of sneering white men shaking ball bats, iron pipes, and other weapons at their victims, of local police simply watching the violence. These images mirror those of other parts of the world in the last half of the twentieth century, a time when the world's dispossessed demanded justice and freedom. The African American freedom struggle of the 1950s and 1960s linked the segregated South to similar oppression the world over. Violent clashes involving racist attackers, police dogs, clubs, and water hoses in Alabama conjured up images of Johannesburg and Sharpesville. These were times of tremendous fear coupled with great hopes and possibilities.

To stop with this description of Anniston would be incorrect. Out of the ashes of the burning Freedom Riders' bus in Anniston in 1961 came a biracial human relations council and a biracial ministerial alliance to mediate community tensions. Hoping to avoid the violent clashes and bloodshed that had and were occurring elsewhere throughout the South, Anniston's white leaders sought a safer ground, by being willing to work across racial lines with black leaders to end segregation in their community. Consequently, issues of equality and justice were for the most part not fought out in the streets between police and civil rights advocates, but were negotiated in interracial meetings of community leaders. Black citizens marched in Anniston to secure economic and political equality, but they encountered relatively little of the brutality unleashed on the civil rights movement in other cities.

To understand why the Anniston civil rights history described here by Phil Noble was uniquely significant, it is useful to examine the larger context of the movement to dismantle segregation in the late 1950s and 1960s. The bus burning in Anniston occurred as the freedom struggle gained momentum all over the South. At times, it seemed as if the worst conflicts occurred only in Alabama. The violent confrontations, however, also dealt major blows to the racist power structure rooted in segregation and disfranchisement. Both the oppressive system of white supremacy and the challenges to it grew out of the post-Civil War history of the South. Alabama stood out during these years for the dramatic contrasts that marked its regional economies. The state became a center for the industrialization that occurred in the "New South" era of the post-Reconstruction years. Northern steel, coal, iron, and railroad companies moved into towns such as Birmingham, Gadsden, and Anniston to exploit the rich natural resources and the black and white labor force that had to work for whatever wages they could obtain. These areas witnessed some of the fiercest labor struggles in the late nineteenth and twentieth centuries as unionization struck fear among the industrialists. Mine and steel company owners—the "Big Mules"—were especially antagonistic toward any attempts at interracial cooperation among the workers. The industrialists attacked such efforts with private as well as municipal police forces, and with other tactics that exploited suspicion and racism among white laborers.[1]

In contrast, the southern Alabama counties known as the "Black Belt" contained large plantations that were worked by the predominantly African American sharecroppers or tenant farmers. By forcing

---

NAN ELIZABETH WOODRUFF grew up in Alexandria, Alabama, and attended Phil Noble's church in Anniston and later in Charleston, S.C. Like many young people, she was inspired by the courageous acts of those involved in the freedom struggle in Anniston and throughout the South. She is the author of American Congo: The African American Freedom Struggle in the Delta *(Harvard University Press, 2003), and she teaches African American and Southern history at the Pennsylvania State University.*

cropper families to buy their supplies, food, and clothing from the plantation store at usurious interest rates, planters insured that their workers would rarely if ever receive a cash return on their crops. Sharecroppers and tenants thus lived in a world circumscribed by debt peonage, poverty, and violence.

Alabama entered the twentieth century, then, with a regional economy that was characterized in the northern counties by small-scale black and white farmers in the countryside and by mines and mills in the towns and cities, and in the southern counties, by plantations worked by impoverished black and white sharecroppers. The northern counties, with lower percentages of black population, saw more direct competition between black and white farmers and industrial laborers, sometimes leading to violent confrontations. And like the rest of the South, Alabama passed segregation and disfranchisement laws in the early part of the century that stripped all African Americans of their citizenship rights, depriving them of the right to vote, to hold office, and to sit on juries. Jim Crow laws segregated public life, forcing black citizens to attend separate and unequal schools, and to ride in specially designated places on public transportation. Separate water fountains and toilets were among the many markers of white supremacy. Black workers were excluded from government jobs and from skilled or white-collar jobs in local businesses. And when they did work in factories or mines, they worked largely in unskilled jobs for less pay than their white counterparts. Local officials routinely harassed and abused black people and often ignored complaints of crimes that came from the black community. As in the rest of the South, vigilante organizations like the Ku Klux Klan terrorized African Americans with whippings, rape, and murder. In many cases, local sheriffs and policemen, judges, and other officials either belonged to the Klan, or stood idly by as the vigilantes terrorized black people.

State politics reflected the harsh realities of the Jim Crow South. Since Reconstruction, Southern politicians had invoked the fear of "social equality between the races" and miscegenation to get elected to office. By using the most vile language, politicians, especially in the twentieth century, stirred up white citizens' fears and hatred of black people.

Racism and white supremacy was used as a political tool to prevent poor and working class white Southerners from mobilizing around the issues that affected their lives–poverty, inadequate education, low wages, and unskilled jobs. Those who reached across the racial divide to challenge segregation and disfranchisement were called communists or worse.

Few politicians of this vein matched the success of George C. Wallace, who dominated Alabama politics for three decades. The "fighting judge" had vowed not to be "out-niggered" again when John Patterson defeated him in the governor's race of 1958. Wallace lived up to his word, and on winning the governorship in 1962, fanned racial hatred and promised to fight segregation till the end. His 1963 inaugural address left no doubt as to his intentions, vowing "Segregation now . . . segregation tomorrow . . . segregation forever." His speech writer, Asa Carter, was one of the most rabid and dangerous racists in the post-World War II South. Carter was born and raised in Oxford, a town that bordered on Anniston. In the 1950s Carter wrote racist pamphlets and worked as a right-wing radio announcer who attacked Jews, Yankees, and African Americans. Carter was not simply a man of words. In an eighteen-month period beginning in January 1957, he and his followers stoned Autherine Lucy when she sought to desegregate the University of Alabama, assaulted Nat King Cole on a Birmingham stage, beat Birmingham civil rights leader Reverend Fred Shuttlesworth and stabbed his wife, and castrated a black handy man. These were not the last of his offenses.[2] That he was subsequently a speech writer for an Alabama governor indicates how lax the law was in dealing with bigots and thugs. His counterpart in Anniston, Kenneth Adams, participated in some of Carter's activities and engaged in numerous other such acts in his hometown.

Governor Wallace rode to national prominence by defying federal efforts to desegregate schools and public facilities and to register black voters. He stood in the door of the University of Alabama in 1963 to prevent Vivian Malone and James Hood from entering as students. He attacked the federal government and the "limousine liberals" who shaped its policies, insisting that state's rights in segregation trumped U.S. Supreme Court interpretation of the Constitution. In 1965, he unleashed the Alabama State Patrol, under Commander Albert J. Lingo, on the black citizens of Selma and the many other activists who had come from all over the country to help in a voter registration drive. Wallace's actions presented to the world the image of a state where racial hatred and violence seemed unaffected by the struggles for justice that were sweeping the region.

African Americans were not silent bystanders to the outrages of white supremacy and legal segregation. In countless ways they challenged and fought against the humiliations and violence that were inflicted upon them. And especially following World War II, they organized against Jim Crow. Returning veterans who had fought fascism in Europe and Asia in a segregated military returned home to demand democracy and justice in their own country. In towns and cities all over the South, veterans organized to secure the vote and an end to segregation. Backed by a more supportive U.S. Supreme Court that outlawed the white primary and segregation, black citizens pressed the court's decisions on a local level and challenged procedures that disfranchised them and sought to use public facilities that denied them access.

Alabama witnessed some of the fiercest challenges to Jim Crow and disfranchisement and it produced some of the most violent responses to the civil rights movement and the Supreme Court decisions, yet it claimed some of the most significant victories in the freedom struggle. The Montgomery Bus Boycott of 1955–56 drew national attention to the state when the city's black residents decided to walk rather than ride segregated buses. Rosa Parks, E. D. Nixon, Jo Ann Robinson, and many others organized the Montgomery Improvement Association to demand their citizenship rights. That struggle also gave rise to the Reverend Dr. Martin Luther King, whose powerful sermons and speeches would galvanize the conscience of a nation, indeed, of the world. The brave actions of the freedom fighters of Montgomery resulted in a major U.S. Supreme Court decision that ordered the desegregation of municipal public transportation systems.

The successes of the Montgomery boycott inspired others to challenge injustice in their communities. For example, in Birmingham, only fifty miles from Anniston, the Reverend Fred L. Shuttlesworth organized in 1956 the Alabama Christian Movement for Human Rights to mobilize the city's poor and working class African American population. Shuttlesworth drew his support largely from within the black Baptist church where protest was often expressed through the "powerful, driving sound of gospel choir music."[3] The Alabama Christian Movement Choir, led by Carlton Reese, combined freedom songs with gospel hits to produce a "charismatic style of music unique to the civil rights struggle." More so than other local movements, the ACMHR "harnessed a radical interpretation of Christianity to power the movement's militancy." Their meetings resembled religious prayer meetings. Religious fervor and a willingness to engage in direct action distinguished Shuttlesworth's group from others in the state.[4]

Birmingham's white political and economic leaders, in contrast to those in Anniston, fought Shuttlesworth and his followers in their attempts to desegregate public facilities and schools. They continued to rely on the Commissioner of Public Safety, Eugene "Bull" Connor to rein in the protestors. The city experienced numerous bombings and other harassment of black activists. City leaders encouraged, either directly or indirectly by silence, the barbaric tactics of Bull Connor's police force. Religious leaders were no better. When the Council of Methodist Bishops issued a resolution in support of the *Brown* decision, white ministers from Montgomery and Birmingham led the formation of the Association of Methodist Ministers and Laymen to defy their national governing body and the U.S. Supreme Court. The lead organizer for this organization was Olin H. Horton, president of the racist Alabama States Rights Association, while many members came from major companies and businesses in the city.[5] Thus Birmingham's power structure mobilized for massive resistance and the city paid a terrible price for their defiance.

Birmingham emerged as an international symbol of the racism and violence that had defined the civil rights struggle in Alabama. On April 3, 1963, members of the Alabama Christian Movement for Human Rights organized boycotts and sit-ins in major department stores and lunch counters in Birmingham. For the next several days hundreds marched in the city's streets to demand equal opportunity and desegregation. Martin Luther King, Jr., and the Southern Christian Leadership Conference joined the protest, and after defying a court injunction against demonstrations, King went to jail and wrote his famous "Letter from a Birmingham Jail." Connor ordered his police force to attack the marchers with dogs. Photographs of snarling dogs attacking protesters covered the pages of the international press. To the world, Birmingham *was* Johannesburg. Before the demonstrations ended in early May, hundreds of children took to the streets and Connor ordered the use of high-pressure fire hoses against the youth. The images of children struggling to survive the battering streams of water captured the world's sympathy, forcing President John F. Kennedy to finally send a representative to the scene. The violence did not end.

In the fall of 1963, Governor Wallace ordered his troopers to block court-ordered desegregation in four cities, including Birmingham. When two black children entered the Graymont Elementary School, Wallace sent in the National Guard to shut down the school. President Kennedy then federalized the National Guard the following morning, creating at least a semblance of compliance. Eleven days later, on Sunday, September 15, a bomb exploded in the Sixteenth Street Baptist Church, killing four little girls. Bull Connor's police department made no arrests in that violent act, and the lead bomber, Robert Edward Chambliss, would not be brought to justice until 1977; two other Klansmen, Bobby Frank Cherry and Thomas E. Blanton, Jr., were not indicted until 2000. Birmingham continued to represent to the world the fiercest resistance to desegregation and equality. Two years later, marchers from all over the country joined black citizens in Selma to demand their right to vote. The violent clashes between the demonstrators and Wallace's state police kept Alabama in the forefront of world reports on the civil rights movement. This time, President Lyndon B. Johnson backed down Wallace and his thugs and signed into law the 1965 Voting Rights Act, which subsequently changed the face of Southern and U.S. politics.

This is the context within which the Anniston human relations council was formed and operated. Luckily, Anniston did not follow Birmingham's lead in massive resistance. While the city had its Klan members, some on the police force, and even had its version of Asa Carter in the person of Kenneth Adams, the city had other factors that allowed events to go in a different direction. Spurred on by a historically liberal newspaper, the *Anniston Star*, a biracial ministerial alliance, and an African American civil rights group, the Calhoun County Improvement Association, Anniston chose to avoid the violence of other cities.

It is astonishing in light of the defiant stand taken in other Alabama cities that Anniston's elected public officials decided to desegregate public facilities peacefully. And it was impressive that ministers like Phil Noble, William B. McClain, Nimrod Q. Reynolds, George Smitherman, and Alvin Bullen, unlike the Methodists in Birmingham and other cities, worked together to forestall bloodshed in Anniston. The reasons for the city's actions varied from the economic to the religious and moral, but no matter the reason, Anniston in the first five years of the decade of the 1960s largely escaped the racial violence that swept across the state, including nearby Gadsden.

Demonstrations and confrontations did come later, as black ministers, some from the human relations council and the Calhoun County Improvement Association demanded further desegregation, economic equality, and justice. While the human relations council had not solved all the problems before it, the precedent was set to approach these issues through negotiation rather than with police dogs and fire hoses. Avoiding further bloodshed was no small task and the brave actions of those involved in forming the council should not be minimized. Poverty, inequality, injustice, and racism persist to this day. The courageous acts of the human relations council and those who continued the struggle long after 1965 serve as reminders that justice for all Americans is never a given–it is something that has been achieved throughout America's history by the struggles of men and women like those described in *Beyond the Burning Bus*. That struggle is not over.

BEYOND THE BURNING BUS

I

The Anniston Bus Burning

OTHER'S DAY SUNDAY, May 14, 1961, was the day Anniston exploded into national Civil Rights headlines. CBS, NBC, and ABC television networks showed a Greyhound bus burning just outside of Anniston. The sign for our local Mello Dairy was visible to one side. Major newspapers across the nation showed the picture of the bus and related the story.

The Congress of Racial Equality (CORE) had organized a bus trip from Washington, D.C., to New Orleans to test the Supreme Court's ruling on desegregation of interstate travel. Calling themselves Freedom Riders, the CORE activists wanted to compel the federal government to enforce the law. Interestingly, this was not the first such experiment conducted by this organization, which consisted of both black and white members, many with religious and/or peace activist backgrounds. In 1947, CORE had attempted a similar Freedom Ride to test an earlier desegregation order. In the earlier ride, the group had traveled without incident until they reached North Carolina, where they were arrested and jailed. Some CORE members served several months in jail at that time, and their efforts had attracted little attention and had little effect.

Things would be very different this time.

On May 4, about a dozen white and black men and women boarded two buses, a Greyhound and a Trailways bus that would make their way through Virginia, North Carolina, South Carolina, Georgia, and into

Alabama, before proceeding to Mississippi and Louisiana. The plan was to arrive in New Orleans on May 17, the anniversary of the 1954 Supreme Court's *Brown* ruling on education.

CORE leader James Farmer wrote later, "We were told that the racists, the segregationists would go to any extent to hold the line on segregation in interstate travel. So when we began the ride I think all of us were prepared for as much violence as could be thrown at us. We were prepared for the possibility of death."[1] Knowing the danger they faced, several of the Freedom Riders left behind letters to their families in case the worst happened.

Though the Ride was well-publicized and it was known all along the route when the Freedom Riders were coming, there were only occasional scuffles as the integrated group used bus terminal restrooms and lunch-rooms in Virginia and the Carolinas. They reached Georgia without serious incident. On Sunday, May 14, the thirteen riders divided into two groups to travel west from Atlanta to Birmingham. The only scheduled stop along the way was at Anniston, Alabama.

A Greyhound bus carrying one group of the Freedom Riders rolled into the Anniston bus station in mid-afternoon when many citizens were finishing a Mother's Day dinner and taking family pictures. But a crowd of Anniston hoodlums, led by local KKK leader Kenneth Adams, met the bus. Of course not only did the Klan know when the Freedom Riders would arrive in Anniston, so did the local police and FBI. In fact, there was a plainclothes law enforcement officer on the bus. Adams and a mob of some two hundred angry people surrounded and attacked the arriving bus, throwing stones and slashing its tires.

The bus raced away, but had to stop six miles west of town on Highway 202 because of the now-flat tires. The driver quickly fled. A large convoy of cars and pick-up trucks had been pursuing the bus and the mob, armed with chains, clubs and iron pipes, again surrounded the vehicle and began smashing its windows. Someone tossed in a firebomb. The passengers scrambled out through the door and windows to face the merciless mob, and seconds later the bus burst into flames. The next day its burning image covered the front pages of America's newspapers.

The burning bus, May 14, 1961. Sadly, this may be the most famous photograph ever taken in Anniston.

A Trailways bus carrying the second group of Freedom Riders arrived in Anniston about an hour after the Greyhound bus. Its passengers met an even worse fate. At the station a number of young white men boarded the bus and began beating the Freedom Riders with clubs and Coke bottles. One of the victims was Walter Bergman, a retired professor from Michigan. His beating resulted in permanent brain damage. No attempt was made by police officers to stop the violence.

The booklet *Free at Last* gives a graphic description of the day's violence:

> Ten days into their journey, on Mother's Day, the first bus of Freedom Riders pulled into the terminal at Anniston, Alabama. Waiting for it was a mob of white men carrying pipes, clubs, bricks, and knives. The bus driver quickly drove off, but the mob caught up with the bus again outside the city. They smashed the windows and tossed a firebomb into the bus. As the bus went up in flames, the riders rushed

out into the hands of the mob and were brutally beaten. When the second busload of Freedom Riders pulled into Anniston, eight white men boarded the bus and beat the occupants from the front to the rear. The most seriously injured was Walter Bergman, who was thrown to the floor and kicked unconscious. He suffered a stroke as a result of the beating and was confined to a wheelchair for life.[2]

Thus, Anniston had shown its potential for violence, long before its potential for non-violent settlement of its problems became apparent.

Anniston reacted. Some felt the horror of the tragedy. The attitude of many was, "It's too bad, but they got what they deserved. They asked for it." Others said, "I am not sorry it happened, but I am sorry it happened here." As the city business community became aware of the national publicity that Anniston received as a result of the burning of the bus and the mauling of the Freedom Riders, they became concerned. Such an image would have a negative effect upon future businesses and industries that might have considered locating in Anniston.

But to some, one realization came clearly into focus: Anniston had the capacity for racial violence that was equal to any other community in the South. That is why Mayor Claude Dear later said to me as he asked me to become chairman of a bi-racial Human Relations Council, "Phil, if the racial situation can be solved without violence in Anniston it can be solved anywhere in the nation. I know Anniston and I know its capacity for violence." What follows is the story of what happened after the burning of the bus on a Mother's Day Sunday afternoon in the beautiful Southern town of Anniston, Alabama.

2

Beginning Years

T HE PSALMIST'S DESCRIPTION of Jerusalem, "beautiful for situation," is appropriate to Anniston, Alabama. The small city is located at the southernmost tip of the Blue Ridge Mountains. Nestled in a valley that runs north and south, its residential area climbs up the slope to the east and spills over into another valley with the beautiful and rhythmic Indian name of Choccolocco. To the west the rolling hills contain the mills and factories that have historically given Anniston more of an industrial base than is common in Alabama cities of comparable size. To the north is Fort McClellan, the long-time U.S. Army complex that served as the primary location of the Women's Army Corps (WAC) and at one time housed the Army's Chemical School. To the south is the old, smaller town of Oxford.

Anniston (population thirty-five thousand) is located on the direct route between Atlanta and Birmingham, just off Interstate 20 about one hundred miles west of Atlanta and sixty miles east of Birmingham. Anniston was founded in the early 1870s by an English family as an industrial town making "soil pipe," a terra cotta product used in buildings and drainage construction. At one time Anniston was known as the Soil Pipe Capital of the World.

The main street was named for this family, whose surname was coincidentally the same as mine. Noble Street thus had no connection with me, but I rather enjoyed the coincidence. Friends who came to visit

An overlook of the city of Anniston as it appeared in the 1950s–'60s.

us after we moved to Anniston would sooner or later notice the street's name and comment. I took a sly pleasure in replying, "I tried to get them not to change the name to Noble Street!"

Noble Street was the dividing line between the eastern and western parts of the city. Kipling's comment that "East is east and west is west and never the twain shall meet" was an apt description of Anniston. Those who worked in the foundries, textile mills, and other manufacturing plants generally lived on the West Side. This was true of both black and white residents. The East Side was almost entirely residential. Those living there were the top managers of the industries, the professional people, and those generally called "white collar" workers.

The views by day and night from the mountain on the East Side were spectacular. At night the lights of the city filled the valley like sparkling diamonds. Anniston was a city of great wealth and much of it was concentrated on the East Side.

The only blacks who lived on the East Side were servants who lived, in a holdover from the old days, on the alleys at the backs of the residences. By the late 1950s and 1960s these situations were rare. I did get to know a servant named "T Ball" who lived behind the house next door to the Presbyterian manse, where my family lived. I never heard anyone say what "T" stood for, if indeed it stood for anything. T Ball was a remarkable person who became the custodian of the First Presbyterian Church and he worked at the church during all the time of the racial strife in the community. He was of the "old school," and we never once discussed what was going on in the community or my role in it. But I had an extremely high regard for T Ball and I think the feeling was mutual.

When I came to Anniston in 1956, Quintard Avenue, two blocks east of Noble, was a beautiful avenue of shaded oaks with a center island. Then it was largely residential, but businesses were already beginning to encroach. The First Presbyterian Church was located on Quintard, in a very old and odd-looking building that no longer stands. Dr. S. T. Meherg of the congregation had left a sizable sum in his will for the building of a new church. When he died in 1958, the church began designing and building a new sanctuary and educational building. It took more than three years to build the new church, a period that overlapped the most critical years of racial tensions. Meanwhile, the old church building was sold to the Alabama Power Company, which demolished it to erect its new facility.

The move of a church from an old location to a new one usually produces some strain and differences of opinion within a congregation. In our case, First Presbyterian met in a junior high school for two years while the new church was being built; this presented some interesting challenges, but otherwise my beginning years in this six-hundred-member congregation were not unusual.

The early years were ones of basic ministry. A morning and an evening service every Sunday and a family night supper service every mid-week gave much opportunity for preaching and interpreting the Word of God. As I reviewed my sermons from this period, in preparation for writing this book, I found no special emphasis on race relations, nor any noticeable avoidance of the subject. Over and again the basic application

Above, the old First Presbyterian Church in Anniston. Left, an artist's drawing of the new First Presbyterian Church, erected in 1964 while Phil Noble was pastor.

of the Gospel was made to our attitudes and relationships to others, including toward the Negro race with whom Southern whites have been so inextricably bound up.

Perhaps two things happened during these years of preaching and pastoral ministry. One was the development of love and trust between pastor and people. I came to deeply love this congregation. I had come to Anniston from the Second Presbyterian Church of Greenville, South Carolina. When I left Greenville, I knew I was leaving a church with many fine and dedicated people. Naturally, I wondered about the quality of Christian faith I would find in Anniston. I soon learned the validity of John Calvin's observation that God has God's own in every place; indeed this was so in Anniston. The other thing that may have been happening was the laying of a good basic foundation for understanding the Christian attitude about race. The first few years I was in Anniston were not years of great crises in race relations; therefore, it might have been possible to plant truth in a way for it to take root, before the issues became so volatile that people could not hear.

Yet I later found it remarkable that I did not know any black ministers during my early years in Anniston. Not a single one. Such was the separation of the black and white churches. Blacks and whites often worked together in filling stations, mills, foundries and restaurants. Many white families had what they felt were close and good personal relationships with maids and yardmen who had worked for them for years. But in Anniston, as in most other Southern towns, there were almost no relationships between blacks and whites in a situation where the two were viewed as equals. There was rigid segregation in the churches as well as in the schools. No congregations had both black and white members. Black ministers had their ministerial associations across denominational lines and white ministers had their ministerial associations across denominational lines, but neither association crossed racial lines. In all these respects, Anniston was no better or worse than any other Southern city or town of the time. This was just how things were.

Of course, change was about to come, in interesting and dramatic ways, and provide a beginning to a complicated and sometimes dangerous process that unfolded in unexpected ways in the months and years ahead. Had I known all that was to happen, I might have been afraid!

3

Early Bridges

I N ANNISTON, as in most of the South, there were two worlds: one of the white people and one of the black people. There was interaction between white and black individuals in the workplace and marketplace and on the street, but each lived in their different worlds and there was little communication across the chasm of segregated Southern culture, custom, and law.

Communication between the two worlds in Anniston started very quietly and simply. In a letter he sent me in 1991, the Rev. William B. (Bob) McClain, then the pastor of Haven Chapel Methodist Church, described that beginning:

> I remember so well, Phil, as if it were yesterday that my [white] Methodist brethren (there were only men in the pulpits then) would not even give me an appointment or allow me to come to their office. You alone, at first, were willing to hear us out. I remember how Nimrod [the Rev. Nimrod Q. Reynolds, then and still pastor of the Seventeenth Street Baptist Church] and I laid the case of the racial situation in Anniston before you: the low-paying jobs, the treatment of black employees in janitorial and other positions of low esteem, the police brutality, the false arrests, the harassment of black people in general, the injustice to not register black people to vote, the segregation and its indefensiveness in the light of the constitution and Gospel, etc., and I

remember you [saying], "Brothers, let's have a word of prayer." And you prayed like I had never heard a Southern white man pray—and you cried as you prayed—and I had never seen a Southern white man cry about anything that related to black people and justice. Nimrod and I cried, too. And we moved from there. That is where the movement for change in Anniston came from. Nimrod and I left the First Presbyterian Church convinced we had met one white Christian and our hopes were renewed.[3]

That encounter recalled by Bob McClain, who was a tall, thin, and light-skinned twenty-four-year-old minister in his first pastorate, took place in 1962. It was quite obvious that he was very bright and well-educated and he spoke easily in a straightforward manner. I am struck now by Bob's recollection that the two black ministers and I, a white minister, all sons of the same South and children of the same God, wept together. I do not specifically remember crying during that meeting, but the issues Bob, Nimrod, and I had begun that day to try to get our arms around were enough to make one weep. They were issues that could be faith-shaking or faith-affirming, depending on what one did with them. My own emotions have always run close to the surface. I feel things deeply and I often show tears of joy or sadness. Tears would have been an appropriate response in such an emotionally laden situation.

Sometime after that meeting, I answered the telephone and heard the voice I would come to know so well over the years, that of Nimrod Reynolds, pastor of the Seventeenth Street Baptist Church. When I first met him, he was thirty-one years old and gave the appearance of a strong, solid person of medium height and build with dark skin. He talked rather softly, with hesitation now and then in his voice. He was an experienced and capable minister who seemed comfortable in that role.

He said, "There are several of us black ministers who feel the need to talk. We would like to have two or three white ministers meet with two or three of us to talk. Would you be willing to meet with us?"

I answered, "Yes, I will be glad to do so. When do you want to meet?"

He suggested the next Tuesday at 10 A.M., at his church

The 17th Street Baptist Church, as it looked in 1963.

"Let's see," I replied. "Obviously your church is on Seventeenth Street."

"Yes, on the west side," he said, assuring me that it would be easy to find. (Anniston was and is, in fact, easy to navigate. Its streets are numbered—First, Second, Third, etc.—and run east and west, while the named avenues run north and south.)

That conversation is revealing as to where we were and how far we had to go. Though I had been in Anniston for six years, I had only recently met Nimrod Reynolds, and he was perhaps the most prominent black minister in town. Furthermore, I did not even know the exact location of his church.

The fact that he suggested meeting at his church was not just because he had issued the invitation. There was more to it than that. In those days it was all right for whites to visit black churches, but it was not all right for blacks to enter white churches. That was rigidly the case where worship services were concerned. White people did not ordinarily attend black churches, but on the few occasions when they did, they were always welcomed, were given the seat of honor, and were publicly recognized from the pulpit with an invitation to return at any time. Black people never, ever attended regular worship services in white churches, with the infrequent exceptions of funerals and weddings when a long-time and loved black servant might come and sit with the white family, truly sharing the family's sorrow or happiness. But that was the extent of blacks' attendance at white churches.

So when Nimrod Reynolds suggested his church as the place to meet, he knew that would be safe. He did not and could not know whether his small group of black ministers would be welcome in my church or some other white church. Though he and Bob McClain had already come to talk with me earlier at my church, on that occasion they were coming as individuals meeting a white individual, not to have a "meeting" of blacks and whites. This context to our early talks is but one small example of the deeply entrenched segregation system that pervaded the deep South. It was not a matter of laws. Though many Southern cities had such laws, in Anniston there were no local statutes forbidding such mixing. Instead there were clear customs and mores, and they were far more difficult to change than laws.

It was no wonder that the black ministers, leaders in their communities, were eager to talk to any white leader who seemed willing to listen. They and their people had suffered under segregation for generations. Now, at the beginning of the 1960s, there was a stirring of hope among blacks all through the South that changes could come.

We were now eight years past *Brown v. Board of Education,* six years past the Montgomery Bus Boycott, and five years past Little Rock's Central High School crisis. The sit-ins that began spontaneously at the Woolworth's lunch counter in Greensboro, North Carolina, in February 1960 had resulted in the organization a few months later of the Student Non-Violent Coordinating Committee. SNCC, as it was known, then helped bring about other sit-ins and boycotts throughout the South as well as in some Northern cities. In November 1960, John F. Kennedy was narrowly elected President after a campaign in which he made a well-publicized phone call of support to Coretta Scott King, whose husband, Martin Luther King, Jr., had been jailed on trumped-up charges. Civil rights activists lost no time in implementing strategies to test a new administration that was apparently more friendly to black causes. One of the first tests touched Anniston directly—the Freedom Rides of May 1961, which we read about in the first chapter. By 1962, on-going demonstrations led by King in Albany, Georgia, had been going on for a year. And things were already heating up in Birmingham.

Like most white people of any sensitivity, I was aware of all these developments. Yet they were not directly a part of my day-to-day existence as they were for my new black friends and fellow pastors. While injustices were as severe in Anniston as they were in Albany and other Southern towns, little if anything, had been done in Anniston to bring about changes. As black leaders locally met with and had conversations with black leaders elsewhere, they would inevitably be asked, "What are you doing in Anniston?" The time was right for something to be done in Anniston, and Nimrod Reynolds and Bob McClain knew it.

It may be difficult for those who have come to maturity after the 1960s to realize how deeply segregation pervaded every aspect of Southern life. Whites accepted segregation as "the system." Most blacks also accepted it, but with resentment. They acquiesced because it had "always been that way" and because they had to live and work under it. They also knew from painful experience that the system of segregation could be and usually was brutal to those who challenged it.

Schools and churches were segregated. "Public" libraries and "public" parks were not public at all. Blacks and whites could share not even beaches, much less swimming pools. No stores, grocery, department, or stores of any nature had black clerks, unless the stores were black-owned, and there were not many of these. Banks and professional offices such as doctors, dentists, and lawyers never had black secretaries or office workers. Almost all had black janitors and cleaning people. Similarly, most white churches employed blacks as janitors, maids, and cooks, but never in the office or any other church position.

Blacks worked in the fields, in the factories and mills, but in unskilled jobs at the lowest end of the pay scale and even then at a lower pay scale than a white working on the same job. Service station jobs were available

The Calhoun County Courthouse in Anniston, 1963.

for the changing of tires and other menial work. Domestic or yard work in homes gave employment for many. Other than employment of this nature, the only opportunities for the most part were in teaching in black schools, preaching in black churches, or becoming lawyers or doctors with black clients or patients. In rare cases, in isolated rural communities where there were few if any white doctors, a black doctor in such a place might have white patients.

Hotels, motels, and restaurants were closed to blacks unless they were black-owned. Blacks traveling through the South had to carefully plan their trip if they hoped to find a place to spend the night or to eat or sometimes even to use a toilet. Often, when a white family took a black maid with them on a trip, when they stopped along the way to eat, the maid remained in the car and a member of the family brought her something to eat. Some restaurants did have a service window on the side or back where a black person could buy something to eat and have it handed out to him or her.

The discriminatory practices against blacks in public transportation, voting, and education are well known. These were the areas around which the major civil rights issues were fought.

However, the system contributed in many other ways to poor self-esteem for blacks and to the notion of racial superiority for whites; both falsehoods were tragically destructive. Blacks were expected to come to the back door, never the front, when visiting the house of a white family. Blacks, even the most distinguished or elderly, were never addressed as Mr. or Mrs., but by given names only. Although grown black men were routinely called "boy," blacks could never call a white person by his or her first name, even if the black involved were much older than the white, as in the case of an older black person calling a white child "Miss" or "Mister." These and other customs of segregation were so deeply imbedded in the system that they were an unconscious and unquestioned way of life for whites and had to be accepted, though with resentment, by blacks.

The resulting unequal status was seen also in the criminal justice system: crimes committed against blacks by whites were overlooked or resulted in light punishment, while crimes committed against whites by blacks resulted in swift and severe punishment.

Thus, it was not surprising that the black ministers, who were leaders of their people, wanted to talk. In retrospect, I wonder only how they had waited so long.

SO, WE MET and began to talk. Present for our first gathering in addition to Nimrod Reynolds and myself were two other black ministers, Bob McClain, pastor of the Haven Chapel Methodist Church, and George Smitherman, pastor of the Mt. Calvary Baptist Church. Another white minister, Alvin Bullen of the Grace Episcopal Church, made a fifth. The result of our first meeting was nothing more than recognition by us all that we needed desperately to build some bridges of communication. We needed it and our communities needed it, if we were ever to deal with our problems without violence. All over the South the civil rights movement was stirring and we all knew we could not avoid such stirrings in Anniston. In fact, while we wanted to avoid violence, none of us wanted

Grace Episcopal Church, Anniston, 1960.

to avoid the issues. The Christian faith required that we deal with these issues in the name of Christ, for the sake of a people who had suffered unjustly for too long.

I felt that I had been instructed by the Christian Faith as a minister of the Gospel of Jesus Christ. This was not by "proof texts" by which it is said; "One can prove anything by the Bible." There are some strong texts such as that which the Apostle Paul wrote in Galatians 3:28: "There is neither Jew nor Greek, there is neither slave nor free, there is neither male or female, for you are all one in Christ Jesus." (RSV) It is also written in Acts 17:26: "And He has made from one blood every nation of men to dwell on all the face of the earth." (New King James Version). But there are also texts that condone slavery. Ephesians 6:5: "Slaves, be obedient to

those who are your earthly masters." Though there are no direct references to segregation, except the command for Jews to be separate from
other races, if in the Bible slavery is approved, then segregation can be
seen as a lesser evil, and by inference is approved by the Bible. Bible-
quoting segregationists and white supremacists sometimes made this
argument.

The Christian Faith instruction to which I refer was not by such texts,
but by what I perceive to be the heart of Christianity: the spirit and love
of Jesus Christ. Can one really imagine that Jesus would think less of a
child because he or she was black? How could I, as a minister of Jesus
Christ, approve and support a system that denigrated people because of
their race when Jesus was receptive of all people, especially the outcasts?

The Christian Church has not always been clear about its role in
relation to slavery or segregation. The Presbyterian Church in the South
during the period before and after the Civil War was in a predicament
regarding slavery. The Church and many of its ministers could not
condone slavery, but it was difficult for them to oppose the practice in the
Confederate States. Therefore the Presbyterian Church developed the
doctrine of "The Spirituality of the Church," by which it was meant that
the Church was to deal only with "spiritual" matters, such as worship,
Bible Study and Prayer, and not be involved in what was considered
social and political matters. In that way the Church sought to get off the
hook regarding slavery. This way of thinking greatly influenced the
Church in the South when segregation/integration became an issue. For
the Presbyterian Church this was a turn away from its long history going
back to John Calvin in Geneva, Switzerland, and John Knox in Scotland,
both of whom were greatly involved in the issues of society and its ills.
However, it must be said that in the Civil Rights struggle the Presbyterian Church as a denomination took a stand against segregation, while
many of its members adopted the "Spirituality of the Church" attitude.

Somewhere along the way the influence of the spirit of Jesus Christ,
and my association with some strong and effective ministers, who saw the
role of Christian leadership was to be involved in the struggle against the
ills and injustices of mankind, led me to work for racial justice.

So, we who had similar goals agreed to meet again and again. We arranged a meeting of the black ministerial association with the white ministerial association. Where did the meeting take place? In one of the black churches, of course!

Small as these steps were, we had made a beginning. Soon, the two groups were meeting regularly about once a month and shortly thereafter we began to rotate the location of the meetings between the white and black churches. The meetings dealt with common concerns of all of the ministers, but there was always a discussion of what was happening in the community as it related to the two races. Over the months of our meetings, some ministers became more interested and others less so, to the point of no longer attending. Finally, the two ministerial associations merged into one organization. That major step indicated a new level of trust between the black and white ministers who were participating in our meetings. However, because the black ministers felt they had to address so many problems, they continued to meet separately as well.

After our associations merged, the Anniston community showed some interest—not all of it positive. Our ministers' group had begun to speak out in opposition to Ku Klux Klan activities, which drew a critical response back toward us. Some of us began getting telephone calls, but they were not yet as threatening as they later became. It was at this time that Charlie Keyes, of whom I will say more later, emerged as a self-appointed spokesman for segregation, opposing any apparent community step toward integregation. Keyes was a Northerner, but he had taken up the banner of the "Southern way of life," which he advocated in a memographed sheet called "The Keyes Report." Tall, thin, and graying, Keyes could often be seen wearing his wide-brimmed western-style hat distributing copies of his sheet up and down the streets of Anniston.

Statements by the Ministerial Association were published in *The Anniston Star,* causing not only the community but also state authorities to take notice. We emerged from one of our association meetings at the Trinity Lutheran Church on 10th Street on the east side of town to find a highway patrolman across the street taking pictures of us. So far as I know, not a single minister tried to avoid having his picture taken and thus escape notice as someone to be watched by state law enforcement.

As the racial conflicts spread and intensified in 1962, George Wallace was loud and vociferous about his stand for segregation. Having been defeated in his race for governor in 1958 by John Patterson, who won with strong KKK support, Wallace vowed that he would not be "outniggered" again. Miller Sproull was elected to the Anniston City Commission on August 21, 1962, as Finance Commissioner. According to a friend of his, he was considering the possibility of running for governor of Alabama at some future time. He went to California with George Wallace to attend a conference. Miller recalls two things from that trip. George Wallace lost his billfold containing his money and his credit cards and Miller let him put his charges on his credit card, with Wallace indicating that he would pay him back. He never did. The other thing Miller recalled quite vividly was that over and over again Wallace said to him, "The only way you will ever do anything in politics is to 'outnigger' everybody else." Miller indicated that Wallace seemed almost totally consumed with a harsh and mean-spirited attitude. Attitudes such as this by Alabama's political leaders gave support to the already generally strong commitment to segregation by the white population in general. In Anniston, it stengthened whites' resistance to our efforts to establish good communications across racial lines, that we hoped would lead to peaceful solutions to problems that were causing serious conflicts in other southern communities.

IT WAS DURING this period of time that I grew by leaps and bounds in my understanding of the problems faced by black people and of the relevance of the Christian faith to them. I am a native Southerner, from genera-tions of Southerners. My immediate family migrated to Mississippi from South Carolina in the early 1800s. In South Carolina, my family had been an important part of the state's history back to the American Revolution, in which my great-great-grandfather, General Andrew Pickens fought. Two of his descendants had been governors of South Carolina, one during the Civil War. Edward Noble, a relative, had made the motion in the South Carolina Assembly for secession in 1860. My grandfather fought in the Civil War and was one of three survivors from his regiment in the battle of Shiloh.

My father, William Alexander Noble, was born in 1865, the year the war ended, and he grew up during Reconstruction. As a young man he was a constable (somewhat like an assistant sheriff) in the area of Learned, Mississippi, our hometown. Though Reconstruction officially ended in 1877, its issues were far from settled during the late 1800s when my father was constable. Stories of his courage were part of the oral history of my family. One in particular stands out. He had arrested and sent a man to jail for some crime. The man vowed that when he got out he was going "to kill Will Noble." Later my father received word that the man had been released from jail in Raymond, Mississippi, and was headed to Learned on the train on a certain day "to kill Will Noble." Learned was a village of fewer than two hundred population. It had one unpaved street with a few stores on either side of it, and the train depot was at one end of the street. When the train pulled in, the man planning to kill my father got off and started walking up the street. There stood my father in the middle of the street with his pistol at his side. While the Learned citizens looked intently out of the store windows to see what was going to happen, my father said, "I understand you have come to Learned to kill me. Well, here I am." The man, knowing that if he had made one false move my father would have shot him on the spot, quickly turned and got back on the train. This was in the late 1800s, but it was like an authentic Wild West drama!

I myself was raised on the farm out from Learned, Mississippi. (Willie Morris, in his book, *My Mississippi,* describes Learned as a "a rambling little town in Hinds County, set in woodlands and pasture that reminds me of New England.") I knew well the sharecropper society. Several black families were sharecroppers on our farm. I played with the children of the sharecroppers. My brother, William, fourteen months older than me, and I had a special black friend who was our age. He had the unusual name of Lysandas. He was killed in World War II. I remember how as boys we would wrestle and sometimes hit one another. The ingrained black-white culture was such that William and I might hit Lysandas, but he would not hit us in return. Both he and we felt it would be out of place for him to do that. It is but a small symbol of the relationship that existed, even in our close boyish friendship.

Southern culture and society was what I breathed and lived. It was not that I accepted or rejected it. I thought no more about it than the air I breathed. But in retrospect, I am aware that as a child I felt compassion for those black children on the farm; I knew they would never have the opportunities that I would have as a white child.

Also, I had the benefit of a seminary education. I had been exposed to the ethic of the Christian Faith. It had been my privilege to be associated with some especially fine, progressive, and sensitive ministers. I had been exposed to much that had raised my awareness of a Christian view of race relations.

I had another advantage in having been elected to the board of directors of Stillman College in Tuscaloosa, Alabama. Stillman was a historically black college but it had, as did most black colleges and universities, an interracial faculty and board. Attending the board meetings and being exposed to black board members and black faculty members was a wonderful experience for me. Especially meaningful were the meals we shared sitting together at the tables. Up to that time, I had not eaten at a table with a black person. This was not unusual in the segregated culture of the South. Most Southern white people had never eaten at a table with a black person, and conversely, most black people had never eaten at the table with a white person. But I was given this special opportunity to have an experience that helped me grow out of my racial prejudice. I well remember how ambivalent I was at the time. I knew in my mind that it was right to be at the table with black people as equals, but I had to deal with my emotions or feelings. This was because of my having lived as long as I had in the segregated culture, unconsciously breathing in its attitudes. Even while I was at the table, I remembered the time on the farm in Mississippi, my brother and I when we were six or seven years old, went into the house of one of our sharecroppers. We were offered a piece of cornbread and we ate it.

Though we had a black cook at our house, this cornbread tasted bad, not because it *was* bad, but because we knew we didn't eat in black folks' houses. Strange as it may seem, I can recall the taste of that cornbread to this day. Because of the Stillman experience, I grew in my emotions and feelings as my racial prejudice began to melt away. Unfortunately, few of my Southern white contemporaries had such opportunities or were open to them.

I HAD NOW COME to know Nimrod Reynolds, Bob McClain, and George Smitherman quite well. I had three small children, and I knew they each had youngsters. My family took a vacation to Florida and we were having a wonderful time. One night in our small quarters, my children were asleep, two on a bed and one on a sofa. I gazed at them with a father's love, thinking that I would do everything in my power to keep them from harm and to give them every opportunity to be and do what they wanted in life. Suddenly, it struck me like a lightning bolt! My friends, Nimrod, Bob and George loved their children, too, and I imagined their desire to keep their children from harm and to give them full opportunities. Sadly, I knew that Southern society, as it was, meant they might never have a chance for their full opportunities. I grieved for the pain and hurt those fathers must feel when they gazed at their sleeping children as I was at mine that night. I realized deep in my heart and soul that Southern life as it then existed simply was not right. It could not be justified on the grounds of morality, or on the grounds of fairness and justice, much less on the grounds of Christian faith.

Difficult days were coming, and I knew it. I also knew that not only could I no longer be a part of condoning what segregation was doing to Negroes, but that I must do what I could to apply Christian principles to the crucial racial issues of the day. I foresaw that that commitment would bring some difficult and threatening challenges in the future, a future that was moving rapidly toward me.

4

Changing the Patterns of Segregation

T
HE SEGREGATION SYSTEM grew out of America's bloody Civil War and its difficult aftermath. It had long since settled its cloud on the South and it remained until my adult years. When white and black southerners got up in the morning, it was there. When they went to bed at night, it was there. For the first half of the twentieth century, it was, more or less, taken for granted by whites and blacks. There had been occasional eruptions by individuals, or by small groups of people, and there were those that spoke out against the segregated system, but it took two world wars and a great depression to shake the foundations of Jim Crow.

(For my younger readers, Jim Crow was a term that referred to the second-class treatment given to blacks under segregation. Some historians attribute the origins of the term to an old black minstrel song.)

What caused the rising up against the system in the 1950s and 1960s? Why then? The elements and interactions of elements that cause a significant change within a social system are hard to pin down. However, there were some major developments that combined to bring about the assault on the patterns of segregation at this time.

FIRST WAS WORLD WAR II. The whole nation, black and white, male and female, majority and minority, worked and served and sacrificed together to win the war. When the war was over, they all went back to civilian life, but the war had changed many people. Black soldiers had fought and risked their lives and died, just as white soldiers had. Blacks had helped to save America—their country—and had helped democracy triumph over facism and nationalist socialism in Europe and Asia. When these black veterans returned, they were "hit in the face" with the old patterns of segregation and discrimination. Many of them were not going to take it! The story of the black soldier, Johnnie Holmes, told in Tom Brokaw's book, *The Greatest Generation,* gives a cameo of incidents that were repeated many times over in various and sundry ways. Johnnie Holmes was one of 1.2 million black Americans who were in uniform during the war. He was one of 10 percent of these who saw combat. He was in training in Louisiana proudly wearing the uniform of the United States Army:

> At the end of basic, Holmes was sent on to Camp Claiborne, Louisiana, to begin his training as a tanker. By now Holmes and the other black soldiers had weekend passes, but even though they wore the uniform of the United States Army and even though they were prepared to give their lives in defense of their country and for the cause of freedom and against the fascist juggernaut rolling across Europe, the racial wounds depeened. Whenever they accidentally strayed into all white neighborhoods they were met with anger and derision : "Hey, boy, what you doin' here? Git outta here, nigger."[4]
>
> Holmes and his fellow black tankers were shipped out for Europe as the 761st Tank Battalion. They were quickly in the thick of battle in the final drive across Europe toward the heart of Germany. They were in combat for 183 straight days, including the worst of the Battle of the Bulge, the ferocious fight through the winter of 1944-45 in the forests of Belgium. They were praised by General Patton and the other commanders of the infantry units they were supporting, but they could not fully escape the racial insults, not even there. Holmes remembers coming back from battles, their tank battered and bloodied by the loss of their comrades, and hearing white soldiers tell Belgium villagers, "Those niggers ain't up there. They're just bringing the tanks up for the

white boys to use." In fact, Holmes and the others in the 761st were face-to-face with death every day.[5]

[When the war was over], Holmes went looking for work. He was now a twenty-five-year-old-battle-scarred veteran, down to ninety-eight pounds as a result of lingering problems from injuries suffered when he was hit by shrapnel from land mines. It was Johnnie Holmes's first stop after getting out of uniform. As soon as he entered the office [to apply for a job], he remembers vividly to this day, the woman in charge of hiring looked up and said, "What are you doing here? We don't hire niggers. Get outta here."[6]

Then Brokaw adds the quintessential words: "Welcome home, Sergeant Holmes!"[7]

Similar incidents happened all over, and probably more often in the South than anywhere else. Edward Wood and his three brothers grew up in the country in Clay County and were in Anniston when they were drafted for service in WWII. One was in the Army, one in the Marines, and Edward and another brother were in the Navy. The Marine brother was in the force that secured Guam. The Army brother was on Guam and Edward himself was on ship off the coast of Guam when the war ended. Edward relates that when he finished boot camp he came home on his first furlough proudly wearing the Navy uniform. He was greeted by a white man who asked, "Where did you get that uniform? Did you steal it?" He replied, "I didn't steal it. Uncle Sam put it on me." Whereupon the white man said, "Ain't no niggers in the Navy. You better take it off before some white folks take it off you." Edward, feeling real anger and resentment, said, "You are a white man. Why don't you take it off?"

When the war was over the four brothers came back home and were honorably discharged. They were advised to go to their court house and get the discharge recorded in case it was ever lost. When Edward and his Marine brother went to the court house to have this done, the white lady at the desk reluctantly took Edward's discharge papers and recorded them. When his Marine brother, who had been in battles on several Pacific Islands, handed her his papers, she replied, "A stinking nigger

Marine! I wouldn't record your discharge if it never got recorded," and threw his papers on the floor. With great effort Edward restrained his brother, knowing the serious consequences if he had retaliated. Another clerk picked up the papers and recorded the discharge.

Edward relates that after he saw another kind of world while he was in the Navy than he had previously known, he was determined to do what he could to change the segregated society. He participated in one of the early sit-ins, and continued to work for change in Anniston. He was among several Anniston residents recently awarded plaques by the Southern Christian Leadership Conference for their activity in the Civil Rights Movement.

Multiply those experiences a few thousand times, and you have a large number of people who "aren't going to take it anymore." With clear insight, Mayor Claude Dear said, "I knew when the blacks answered the WWII call, things were going to be different when they returned."

THE SECOND FACTOR was the intensifying behind-the-scenes legal maneuvering to combat racial discrimination and injustice. In his book *Civil Rights and Wrongs,* Harry S. Ashmore writes:

> Over two decades litigation initiated by the National Association for the Advancement of Colored People had undermined the states rights policy that condoned apartheid. The series of cases that culminated in the Supreme Court's 1954 ruling against segregation in public education committed the federal government to protect the civil rights of blacks wherever they were denied by the action, or inaction, of local authorities. Assurance of this kind of support released the pent-up resentment that sent masses of blacks into the streets to challenge Jim Crow.[8]

THIRD, THE RACIAL BARRIER was broken in sports. Jackie Robinson played for the Brooklyn Dodgers in 1947. That was a crack in the door that was gradually pushed open until black athletes took their place in every sport. That was an extremely popular symbol, not only for young black athletes, but for all black people.

FOURTH, TELEVISION came on the scene. When World War II ended, television was just emerging. I remember being in Rich's department store in Atlanta near the end of the war and seeing television for the first time. It expanded rapidly. In a few years, scenes from around the world were seen in nearly every home. This also meant that ideas now spread rapidly. Large numbers of people could be motivated to support a cause. A gross incident of injustice could be displayed to the whole nation. People, both in their needs and causes could see that they were not alone. A small local demonstration could have national impact. Television became a powerful tool in arousing the nation's conscience to Southern injustice. It was a new, fresh and powerful instrument.

FIFTH, PROPHETS of social change spoke out, and leaders came forth. Martin Luther King, Jr., emerged as a dynamic prophet and leader. He seemed to be just right for the rising tide of opposition to segregation and the discrimination it had institutionalized.

SIXTH, THE DECISIONS and stances of the Federal judges in the U.S. Fifth Circuit, especially circuit judges such as Elbert P. Tuttle in Atlanta, Richard Rives in Montgomery, and John Minor Wisdom in New Orleans, and a few district judges such as Frank M. Johnson, Jr., in Montgomery, had significant effect. Their decisions gave bedrock substance to the cultural revolution, which was occurring and ultimately helped to make the difference in the outcome of the struggle. Judge Irving L. Goldberg said:

> Preachers and writers have been preaching and writing for generations that we should do certain things for our brothers and they have been heard but not heeded . . . And that's where the courts come in. The courts not only are heeded, but what's important in their being heeded is the voluntary (public) acceptance that the courts do speak for the moral heights of our society. And when they don't, they forfeit their

responsibility.[9]

The significant role of the judges is clearly indicated in the following passages from *Unlikely Heroes* by Jack Bass:

> In the major cases...that deal with voting, jury selection and school desegregation, the Fifth Circuit [Court of Appeals] created the doctrine that attacked the foundation of an entrenched system of racial discrimination. But the greatness of the Fifth Circuit as a civil rights court derived equally from the combination of its unflagging energy that kept after hundreds of local officials, registration commissions, and school boards who sought to wear down the opposition by fighting every inch of the way and its readiness to ride herd on district judges willing to cooperate with foot-dragging local officials.[10]
>
> . . . Through its civil rights decisions, the Fifth Circuit Court of Appeals perhaps did more than any other institution to transform the South and reshape its attitudes.[11]

SEVENTH WAS THE all-pervasive feeling among black people, and also among many whites, that "the time had come." The injustice and discrimination had gone on too long, and now was the time to dismantle the segregation system. The feeling was now growing that change was inevitable. These feelings were both captured and further promoted by phrases from two songs sung over and over again by thousands in whose hearts hope would not die: "We Shall Overcome" and "Blowing in the Wind."

When these seven factors interacted, bonfires of revolution blazed in community after community in the South, which kept burning and spreading, jumping barrier after barrier, until finally the walls of segregation came tumbling down. This is what was happening in the turbulent events in the South in the 1950s and 1960s. And it happened in Anniston, Alabama, too.

5

The Events of the 1950s and 1960s

T HE SEEDS OF THE SOCIAL REVOLUTION of the 1950s and 1960s were "blowing in the wind" into communities across the entire South. When the conditions were ripe, as described in the previous chapter, these seeds germinated and grew into full maturity. The city of Anniston was no exception, and it was against the backdrop of a decade of growing civil rights activity that the Reverends Nimrod Reynolds and Bob McClain first came to see me, and the movement to work out the racial problems in Anniston in a more civilized and non-violent way began.

The social revolution had been gradually developing since the end of World War II. But the Supreme Court decision of May 17, 1954, in the case of *Brown* v. *Board of Education of Topeka* outlawing segregation in public schools, marked the real turning point. This decision ignited hope in the black community and was a wake-up call to the white community. The Ku Klux Klan had been in existence since Reconstruction, but this Supreme Court decision stimulated the resurgence of the Klan. The white South began immediately to look for ways to resist the Supreme Court decision and to maintain segregation. A resurgence of the Ku Klux Klan was one result. The emergence of the White Citizens' Councils was another. While the KKK generally appealed to the "red-necks" in the south, the White Citizens' Councils often included the leading white citizens of the community. Mississippi newspaper editor Hodding Carter called the Council "the uptown Klan." Harry Ashmore, in his book *Civil Rights and Wrongs,* describes the origins of this phenomenon:

> At Indianola, Mississippi, fourteen leading citizens had "met and counseled together on Black Monday"—that being the day the Supreme Court handed down Brown I. Thus was born the loose confederation of segregationist organizations called White Citizens' Councils that spread across the South in the following months. The first chairman, Robert P. Patterson, a Leflore County planter, condemned the traditional night-riding violence of the past and pledged that the councils' opposition to school desegregation would be carried out by lawful means. The founders' legal expert, Judge Thomas Pickens Brady, specifically disavowed the Ku Klux Klan: "They hide their faces because they do things you and I wouldn't approve of."
>
> What the councils would approve of was spelled out in the wake of Brown II when the NAACP moved to initiate five test cases in Mississippi. At Yazoo City fifty-three black parents petitioned the local school board for an immediate end to segregation, and a mass meeting of white citizens was assembled in the high school auditorium to discuss the matter. Young Willie Morris, a senior at the University of Texas home for summer vacation, recognized all of the dozen prominent men who sat on the platform. "Some of them were fathers of my best friends, men I had known and admired and could talk to on a first-name basis," he wrote in his memoir *North Toward Home.* In the audience he saw his father sitting with a neighbor. And from the back of the hall he heard rebel yells and shouts of "Let's get the niggers!" The chairman quickly stilled the clamor. The white citizens of Yazoo City, he said, would neither commit nor condone violence. He then outlined the procedure to be followed in protecting the Southern Way of Life. Employers of blacks who signed petitions would fire them, and if they were tenants their landlords would evict them. Wholesalers would cut off supplies and credit to the black retailers, and black customers would be turned away by white merchants when they sought to buy goods.[12]

In the companion book to the PBS documentary series *Eyes on the Prize* the comparison is made between the Klan and the White Citizens' Councils:

> The Klan's members were generally poor, rural white men. Wearing white robes and hoods that covered their faces, they set crosses ablaze on the lawns of integrationist "troublemakers." If that tactic failed to intimidate, they resorted to beatings and murder. The Citizens' Councils, which began to proliferate throughout the South, sought to control blacks more through economic reprisals than by violence. One Council leader said that their purpose was "to make it difficult, if not impossible, for any Negro who advocates desegregation to find and hold a job, get credit, or renew a mortgage."[13]

A horrible incident that caught the attention of the nation was the murder in Mississippi of Emmett Till, a fourteen-year-old black youth, on August 28, 1955. *Free at Last*, a history of the Civil Rights Movement and those who died in the struggle, tells the story:

> A magazine writer later paid Milam to describe what happened that night. Milam said he and Bryant beat Emmett Till, shot him in the head, wired a 75-pound cotton gin fan to his neck and dumped his body in the Tallahatchie River. When asked why he did it, Milam responded: "Well, what else could I do? He thought he was as good as any white man." Till's body was found three days later—a bullet in the skull, one eye gouged out and the head crushed in on one side. The face was unrecognizable.
>
> Mose Wright (a 64-year-old farmer and grandfather of Emmett Till's cousin) knew it was Till only because of a signet ring that remained on one finger. The ring had belonged to Emmett's father Louis, who had died ten years earlier, and bore his initials L. T.
>
> Mamie Till demanded the body of her son be sent back to Chicago. Then she ordered an open-casket funeral so the world could see what had been done to Emmett. *Jet* magazine published a picture of the

horribly disfigured corpse. Thousands viewed the body and attended the funeral. All over the country, blacks and sympathetic whites were horrified by the killing. Thousands of people sent money to the NAACP to support its legal efforts on behalf of black victims.

In the meantime, J. W. Milam and Roy Bryant faced murder charges. They admitted they kidnapped and beat Emmett Till, but claimed they left him alive. Ignoring nationwide criticism, white Mississippians raised $10,000 to pay the legal expenses for Milam and Bryant. Five white local lawyers volunteered to represent them at the murder trial. Mose Wright risked his life to testify against the men. In a courtroom filled with reporters and white spectators, the frail black farmer stood and identified Bryant and Milam as the men who took Emmett away. Wright's act of courage didn't convince the all-white jury. After deliberating just over an hour, the jury returned a verdict of not guilty.

The murder of Emmett Till was the spark that set the civil rights movement on fire. For those who would become leaders of that movement, the martyred 14-year-old was a symbol of the struggle for equality."[14]

The White Citizens' Council held a kickoff meeting in Jackson, Mississippi, on July 11, 1954, not quite two months after the Supreme Court decision. It and other forms of resistance rapidly spread across the South.

Meanwhile, civil rights activities were moving just as rapidly. The Montgomery, Alabama, bus boycott began December 5, 1955, and continued until a legal victory ending segregated intracity bus seating was implemented on December 21, 1956. Of course, the boycott was known in every black and white community throughout the nation. It was through the Montgomery Bus Boycott that Martin Luther King, Jr., and Ralph David Abernathy, both pastors of black Baptist churches in Montgomery, emerged as leaders of what was beginning to be recognized as a "movement." Both their homes, and those of other black leaders, including that of the Rev. Fred Shuttlesworth of Birmingham, were bombed.

On November 25, 1955, the Interstate Commerce Commission banned segregation on interstate travel, though the edict had little effect. In February 1956, Autherine Lucy was admitted to the University of Alabama. The State of Alabama outlawed the NAACP in June of that year.

The movement gained momentum in January 1957 with the founding of the Southern Christian Leadership Conference by black ministers from throughout the South; Martin Luther King, Jr., was elected president. The Little Rock, Arkansas, Central High School integration controversy began in August, which brought out federal troops, and lasted until May 1959.

Strife continued and in February 1960 sit-ins began in Greensboro, North Carolina. These spontaneous events led to the organization later that spring of the Student Nonviolent Coordinating Committee (SNCC). While the MLK-led Southern Christian Leadership Conference had consisted mostly of older black ministers, SNCC was an organization of mostly black college students. They were deliberately more activist.

Also in 1960 John F. Kennedy was elected President and a Civil Rights Act was signed that "extended authority to intervene in cases of voting discrimination"[15] and authorized suits against the state. And the earlier ICC ruling barring segregation in interstate travel was upheld by the U.S. Supreme Court. In the early spring of 1961, the civil rights organization CORE (Congress of Racial Equality) planned a test of that Supreme Court decision and of the new Kennedy administration's willingness to enforce it. This test would become known as the Freedom Rides and would directly and significantly affect my adopted hometown of Anniston.

A year-long campaign by the SCLC was launched in 1961 in Albany, Georgia, a town about the size of Anniston, which easily could have been the site of a similar struggle. The University of Georgia admitted blacks for the first time, but not before a riot on January 11, 1962. It was even worse that year at the University of Mississippi (Ole Miss), where two people were killed and 375 injured before James Meredith successfully if temporarily desegregated that institution.

The year 1963 was the most violent yet. Birmingham exploded in April and May, and was rocked with violence culminating in the bombing of the 16th Street Baptist Church and the killing of four small girls. Martin Luther King, Jr.'s famous "Letter from the Birmingham Jail" was written and circulated throughout the nation. Governor George Wallace took his famous schoolhouse stand on June 11th. Mississippi NAACP leader Medgar Evers was assassinated as he was entering his home the night of June 12th. President John F. Kennedy was killed on November 22.

These are just a few highlights, or, most often, lowlights, of the civil rights incidents and activities that were occurring across the country during these tumultuous years. Anniston, of course, was thrust into the spotlight of civil rights by the Freedom Rides of 1961.

This photo depicts a march in Anniston in 1979, but its spirit is reflective of some marches in the 1960s. The Rev. N. Q. Reynolds is on the left front.

6

Anniston Simmers

WITH THE EXCEPTION of the Freedom Riders bus burning in 1961, the racial scene in Anniston had seemed relatively peaceful. However, this was an illusion. The black community was in ferment. They saw television. They read the newspapers. They were keenly aware of the struggles that were occurring in other towns and cities. The winds of change that were blowing over other communities brought their seeds to Anniston. They landed on fertile soil because there had been discontent for a long time.

The actions of the police department were more than an irritation to the black community. And, of course, there were no black officers on the police force. It was difficult for blacks to register to vote. The strong pattern of rigid segregation was to be found in the factories, even the unions, the shops, stores, schools and churches, and in public transportation (buses).

The black community began to stir. They organized themselves into the Calhoun County Improvement Association. They went from door to door in their communities encouraging people to register to vote. Their ministers spoke out, further sensitizing the people to the situations that discriminated against them. Because they saw movement in other communities, they were given hope that changes could be made in their community. They went to the Chamber of Commerce, to stores and places of business urging them to hire blacks in positions other than janitorial and maintenance. They went to the city government and urged the hiring of policemen and firemen.

They met very little positive response.

During this period Southern white churches confronted the question of whether blacks would be seated if they came to the church. The churches in Anniston were no exception. The Session of First Presbyterian Church voted, not unanimously, to seat blacks if they came, and so instructed the deacons who were in charge of ushering. One deacon, a very prominent young man in the community, said to me that he would not seat blacks. I told him not to usher as the Session had set the policy of the church. Even though the Session had voted to seat black visitors, the feeling was that they should be seated at some special place in the church rather than with the other worshippers. The pattern varied in other churches. For example, several black servicemen and women from Fort McClellan came to Grace Episcopal Church and were seated without apparent incident.

The indignities of segregation were manifold and were experienced by every black person in his or her daily life. Edward Wood, a black man, tells of going to the drugstore to get a prescription filled. He had his four-year-old son with him. At that time, the store had a small short-order section. His son, who loved hamburgers, saw them being served and wanted one. As he began to cry, not understanding why he could not have one, Wood took him out without getting the prescription filled. It was a painful and poignant moment for Wood.[16]

Younger readers will not believe this, but in those days full-service gas stations were the norm. The attendant would pump the gas and clean the windshield, check the oil, and sometimes even put air in the tires as part of the routine service. But one black man recounted for me his not untypical experience of pulling into a filling station and buying gasoline. The white attendant not only would not clean the windshield, but with oaths told the man to clean it himself.[17]

That the atmosphere in the community was moving toward violence is illustrated in an incident told by another black man, E. C. Tolbert. He had a white convertible automobile and as he was driving down the street, several white boys threw raw eggs on his car. Tolbert followed them and caught up with them two stoplights later. Tolbert got out with his .44-caliber pistol and pointed it at the boys, saying, "Get out and lick those eggs off my car." The boys did![18]

Everyone sensed that more and greater violence was just below the surface in Anniston as throughout the country.

It was during this period that the white and black ministers began to meet together to try to establish bridges of communication. Eventually the trust level grew until the white and black ministerial groups merged into one ministerial association.

In the city, on April 10, 1962, in the Democratic primary, Claude Dear was elected Mayor, Miller Sproull was elected Finance Commissioner, and Jack Suggs, Police Commissioner. Miller Sproull had put in his campaign material that he was in favor of the city's appointing a biracial committee. He had asked me to help him draft the statement. There was no Republican opposition and the three city commissioners took office on October 1, 1962. That same day the *Anniston Star* ran headlines about the rioting in Oxford, Mississippi, when James Meredith was admitted to Ole Miss. Federal troops had been brought in and Governor Ross Barnett made the statement: "We will not surrender!"

Tension had so mounted in Anniston that on October 23, 1962, Mayor Claude Dear and I, as president of the now interracial Anniston Ministerial Association, issued a joint statement calling for a community-wide prayer event on the following Wednesday. The statement read:

> Our nation under God faces a crisis that concerns the entire world. The risks that are involved for the human race demand that we call upon Almighty God for His mercy and overruling providence. Our nation, recognizing its place under God from Plymouth Rock and Valley Forge to the present crises, has repeatedly called upon God for mercy and direction. Therefore, we, the Mayor of the City of Anniston, and the President of the Anniston Ministerial Association, call the community together in its churches from 12:00 to 12:15 P.M. Wednesday, October 24, for quiet prayer in behalf of our nation and world and their leaders.[19]

Less than a month later, on November 13, 1962, the *Anniston Star* printed the following article:

ANNISTON MINISTERIAL GROUP
ISSUES CALL FOR LAW AND ORDER

Anniston Ministerial Association members Monday called on area residents to meet any school integration crises with Christian standards of responsibility and obedience to law and order. Gov.-Elect George C. Wallace and all state officials were called on to provide the leadership toward avoiding the sort of violence that erupted this fall on the campus of the University of Mississippi. Their measure followed a similar call for civil obedience issued last weekend by the Trustees and Alumni of the University of Alabama where the next college integration crisis may come soon. This unanimous call for peace and civil observance of laws came in this resolution: 'The Anniston Ministerial Association by this resolution respectfully requests that the Gov.-Elect George C. Wallace, and all state authorities seek to avoid the tragedy of Mississippi repeated in any part of the state of Alabama. Our state stands between the two states of Georgia and Mississippi. Both states have faced the problem, which shall be ours. One has handled it by preserving law and order. The other has not. We believe the vast majority of thinking and responsible citizens of Alabama want vigorous leadership in the direction of obedience to the law and avoidance of needless violence. We encourage the people of our community and state who believe in like manner to speak out for the welfare of our state and all its citizens.

In adopting this resolution, we affirm:

1. That neither hatred of fellow man nor violence which stems from it has sanction in the Christian faith.

2. That there may be disagreement concerning laws and social change without advocating defiance and anarchy.

3. That laws may be tested in courts, changed by legislatures, but not ordered by the whims of individuals.

4. That no person's freedom is safe unless every person's liberty is

equally protected.

5. That good will is a matter of the heart and ultimately is dependent upon man's relationship to God.

6. That every human being is created in the image of God and is entitled to respect as a fellow human being with all basic rights, principles and responsibilities.[20]

This was the beginning of late-night telephone calls to my home that increased in number and escalated into threats. Also in November Dr. Martin Luther King, Jr., came to Anniston as part of a tour of Alabama and spoke to about forty people at a luncheon.

Our racial troubles began to have a financial impact on the community. In 1962 the General Electric plant in the Anniston area closed down. The city needed to get more industry and the bus burning in 1961 as well as the continuing activity of the Ku Klux Klan was giving Anniston a bad image. As Anniston's image deteriorated, it became increasingly difficult to get industry, and this fact captured the attention of Anniston's business community.

During all of this period since the Supreme Court's *Brown* decision, the matter of the integration of the schools had been developing. The *Anniston Star* carried a story on February 22, 1963, indicating that the federal government had issued a decision providing for the desegregation of schools at six military bases in Alabama, Georgia, and South Carolina. The Department of Health, Education and Welfare had said: "Children who are required to attend segregated schools do not get a suitable education!"[21] The schools at Fort McClellan in Anniston were among these. I was proud of Kathleen Johnson, a member of First Presbyterian Church who was teaching at Fort McClellan and strongly supported the integration order, though she had to endure criticism.

It was about this time that Charlie Keyes, a native Northerner who now lived in Anniston, became the self-appointed spokesman for segregation. He published a mimeographed periodical called "The Keyes Report" and circulated it through the community. Through it, he constantly stirred the fires of resistance, prejudice and hatred. In addition, as the schools became integrated, he often marched on the sidewalks in front of the schools as the students arrived, carrying signs for segregation and opposing integration. On occasion he would say to my children, Betty, Phillips and Scott: "You are Rev. Noble's daughter," or "You are Rev. Noble's son." But knowing my three children, they were not intimidated! On one occasion as my wife let my daughter Betty out of the car to go to school, as she crossed the street Charlie Keyes shook in her face a sheet of paper calling for segregation while remarking that she was Rev. Noble's daughter. In typical defiance Betty said, "Aw! Shut up!" She had just witnessed a few days before an incident at the high school. Three young black students had put their books on a bench at the entrance of the school and were waiting to go in. A group of hoodlums with lead pipes wrapped in newspaper emerged and attacked the students. They dispersed as Betty ran into the school building to inform the school principal.

Later on, one Sunday morning as I was driving to the church with Phillips in the car, we were talking about what was happening regarding the racial situation. Phillips said, "I am afraid you all are going to get everything done and there will be nothing left for me to do!" I assured him that we would not get it all done, and there would be plenty for him to do.

My good friend Miller Sproull had a hunting lodge down in Georgia across the river from Eufaula, Alabama. Knowing that I enjoyed quail hunting, he would invite me down to hunt with him several times a year. During the fall of 1962 and early winter of 1963 on these trips, we discussed what was happening in the church and community. We talked at length about the need for a city-appointed bi-racial committee. He assured me that the city commission was indeed going to appoint such a committee. I knew he was committed to doing this, but given the situation, proper timing was important. Soon the time came and the Bi-Racial Human Relations Committee was appointed. Mayor Dear noted with some degree of pride and wonder that it was probably the South's first such official biracial committee.

7

The Bi-Racial Human Relations Council

THE WEATHER WAS BEAUTIFUL in Anniston on Mother's Day, May 12, 1963. The sun had risen over 10th Street Mountain on this spring day bringing its warm light to the town in the valley below. The steeples of its churches pointed upward and all through the town, mothers were to be honored and gratitude expressed for them. Worshippers at the many churches would be wearing a red or white flower in recognition of mothers living or mothers dead. How wonderful and peaceful! But this Mother's Day would mark a turning point which would impact the community of Anniston in a remarkable way. The stream of Anniston's history took a turn for good as a result of the actions of a few evil and cowardly men.

May seemed to be a time for racial tensions to escalate. As we have seen, two years to the day earlier, Anniston and Birmingham had been the scene of Mother's Day violence involving attacks on the Freedom Riders. Now, in 1963, because the racial situation in Birmingham was so tense, the military was keeping a close watch on the whole area around Birmingham. A communication dated May 6 to the White House and to the military at Fort McClellan was sent from Major General W. B. Rosson:

> Rumors exist in Anniston, Ala., concerning a possible attempt to integrate the white First Methodist and Parke [Parker] Memorial

Baptist churches, 19 May 63. However, contacts in the Negro community indicate little likelihood of trouble.[22]

The Session (the governing body) of the First Presbyterian Church
had a called meeting Thursday, May 9, to discuss whether to rent its new
educational building to the Anniston Academy, a private school that was
just beginning. For various reasons, the Session decided not to rent the
facilities. Then after the Session had completed its business, E. L.
Turner, Jr., an older and respected elder who was chairperson of the
church's building committee, stated that he had been to Birmingham
that day on business and had found the city in a terrible condition from
boycotts and much violence. He asked that the Session be led in prayer
that Anniston be spared what Birmingham was experiencing. As mod-
erator of the Session, I said we most surely should and would pray to that
effect, but I asked if there was anything else we could do. Then I
indicated that some of us had been urging the city to appoint a Bi-Racial
Committee for some time. Then I asked if the Session knew of any better
thing we could do. I was aware of the fact that some Session members
were opposed to appointment of such a committee. After a long discussion, the members of the Session could not come up with what they
thought was a better alternative. The Session then voted to urge the city
commission to appoint a bi-racial committee. On Sunday morning,
Mother's Day, each without the knowledge of the other, the Rev. Alvin
Bullen of Grace Episcopal Church and I preached sermons urging the
appointment of a bi-racial committee.

With the explosive situation in Birmingham, the racial tension in
Anniston was escalating. The Session of the First Presbyterian Church
having passed the resolution calling for the appointment of a biracial
committee, I felt that an added word from me from the pulpit would give
weight to the Session's resolution. I knew Miller Sproull had wanted for
a long time to appoint such a committee, and fully intended to do so. He
knew that the Mayor was in favor and that Police Commissioner Jack
Suggs was opposed. It was strongly suspected that some police officers
were KKK members. Miller was aware of the possibility that the Police

Department under Jack Suggs might not support the probable recommendations of a biracial committee. If that happened, the creation of a biracial committee might generate chaotic conditions for the community. Miller and Mayor Dear were aware of the potential problems. Therefore the timing of the appointment of such a biracial committee was critical.

I knew Miller would be in church worship on Sunday and I felt a bit badly when I said, perhaps too bluntly, in the sermon that we had been promised over and again that a biracial committee was going to be appointed and yet it had never been done. Miller was much more aware of the need for proper timing than I was. I was unaware of the potential lack of support from the police.

After Church worship on this Mother's Day, church families went home to celebrate the day and honor their mothers. In our own family we always made much over Mother's Day. That day, we had a wonderful dinner and our children, Betty, Phillips, and Scott, gave cards and presents to their mother, expressing their love for her. It was an especially warm family time that lasted until mid-afternoon.

In the late afternoon the telephone rang and I answered. It was Miller Sproull.

He said, "Phil, this is Miller. Have you heard the news?"

I said, "No, what news?"

"The homes of two Negro families and the St. John's Methodist Church in south Anniston were fired into this afternoon by white men using shotguns."

I quickly asked, "Was anybody killed?"

"Fortunately," he said, "no one was killed or injured." Then he added, "We are ready to appoint the biracial committee. Can you meet the Mayor and me at the City Hall tomorrow morning to talk about it? We want you to be the Chairman."

There was a pause before I said anything. It raced through my mind how greatly opposed the white South was to biracial committees. City after city had refused to set up such a committee. The mayor of Jackson, Mississippi, twenty-five miles from my home place of Learned, had sworn he would never appoint a biracial committee. In Birmingham and other cities and towns black leaders had pressed for such committees. Hardcore segregationists usually proclaimed that biracial committees were just the first step to "giving in to the niggers." The appointment of this committee in Anniston would be a signal for the already-active Klan in Anniston to intensify their violence. I immediately realized that the biracial committee itself would be a likely object of the Klan's violence.

I was also aware that I had had much to say about the need for such a committee. Could I now refuse?

I asked Miller what time to be there, he told me, and I agreed.

When I put up the telephone my wife asked, "Who was that?"

"Miller Sproull."

"What did he want?"

"He told me a Negro Church and two Negro homes had been shot into by white men this afternoon. "

Over the weeks and months Betty knew I had urged the appointment of a biracial committee and that Miller and I had discussed it often. I continued, "He said they are now ready to appoint a biracial committee. He wants me to meet with him and the Mayor at City Hall at ten o'clock tomorrow morning. He said they want me to be chairman of the committee."

There was a long pause. We were both a bit naive about the potential danger, but we both knew the threat to all of us, including our three children.

"Are you going to do it?"

"Well, you know I have been urging the appointment of such a committee, and I have had much to say about it in private and from the pulpit. I don't see how I could say no."

Again a long pause. Our family would be at risk. Betty was reared in a good Christian family with a strong sense of right and wrong. If something was wrong, you did not do it. If something was right, you did it. Period.

Then she said, "I think it is right. I am glad you are going to do it."

We talked more about the rightness of the step and the risk of it.

Betty's great-great-grandmother was Agnes Scott, for whom Agnes Scott College in Decatur, Georgia, is named. Agnes's son, Colonel George Washington Scott, Betty's great-grandfather, had founded the college and named it for his mother. Passed down in the family for generations had been a Bible passage that was special to Agnes, Proverbs 3:5-6. "Trust in the Lord with all thine heart, and lean not unto thine own understanding. In all thy ways acknowledge Him and He will direct your paths."

Betty now quoted this verse saying this is what we live by and it will be our strength and guide in this situation. (This is the verse that would give us strength five years later, when our youngest son, Scott, died after an eighteen-month battle with leukemia.) She never wavered or questioned again whether we were doing the right thing.

I LAY AWAKE A LONG TIME Sunday night. So many things flashed through my mind, and some of them lingered a long time. The strongest emotion had to do with my family. Betty was fourteen years old and Phil Jr. would be twelve in less than a week. Scott was eight. Would what I was about to do put them in danger? My wife and I had learned over the years to handle criticism. How would the children react to jabs and comments from their peers, who would echo their parents' racial attitudes? Would there be an adverse effect on their normal development? As it turned out, that was one thing I did not have to worry about. The results in the children's development were not negative, rather very positive. Today in their adult life there is no racial prejudice and this was also the result in the lives of some of those who were friends of theirs during this time.

I thought about my wife, Betty. I knew she was strong and over the years I had observed her letting little personal slights roll off like water on a duck's back. But the coming slights and jabs might not be so little. During the 1950s and 1960s I knew of a number of ministers and their families who had been harassed by the congregation because of their stands on racial issues. Would this now be our lot? The Presbyterian denomination had set up a program for ministers and their families caught in such situations to get support. Would we need it? I speculated that the First Presbyterian Church congregation would not react in such an adverse way. After all the Session, composed of lay representatives of the congregation had just voted unanimously to urge the City to appoint a biracial committee.

My thoughts returned to my earliest days on the farm in Mississippi. In some ways I had come a long way. I thought of the sharecropper families on our farm and the way my brother and I had played with the sharecropper children, with them always "in their proper place." In retrospect I thought about the "traps" they were caught in, with no real hope for them to have a life of opportunity as I would have.

I thought of our black teenage friend, Lysandas, who was always laughing and joking as we played together. I recalled that time when he and I had gone when it was early dark to the hog lot, about five hundred yards back of the house, to feed the pigs.

The pig pen was never very close to the house for obvious reasons. When we returned to the house it was time for Lysandas to go home. He would walk through the lawn in front of the house, down a long well-worn path that led by the cook's house in the far corner of the lawn, and on across the gravel road where he lived with his sharecropper parents.

As he walked out the front gate of the picket fence, he closed it, and started down the path whistling as he went. The family had conceived an idea which they thought would be a good joke. My older brother, Pickens, who had recently finished college and was in his first coaching job in Houston, Mississippi, was at home for a visit. Right by the path in the lawn a large oak tree had fallen some time before. Pickens, with a white sheet over him, laid down behind the log. Just as Lysandas got to the log, Pickens raised up, waved his arms, and let out a yell. Lysandas turned and fled up the path back to our house, hollering to the top of his lungs with fear, sailed completely over the picket fence and lay on the front porch, still screaming and trying to get his breath. Lysandas's father, Ellis (of course I did not know his last name), hearing the screams, came running up to the house. It was a cruel joke, which my family did not mean it to be, as they had tried to get me to walk home with Lysandas so we both would have "the experience." If I had gone it would have been doubtful which of us would have screamed the loudest or run the fastest!

I remembered that some years later Lysandas had made the supreme sacrifice in World War II.

I thought about how segregation had been a part of my growing up years without my having given much thought to it. I thought about how my awareness of race relations had been raised when I was a student at Columbia Theological Seminary. I recalled a somewhat avant garde sermon—for the Deep South—that seminary president Dr. J. McDowell Richards had preached, entitled, "Brothers in Black." I thought of the time I had spent on the Stillman College Board, a predominantly black Presbyterian college in Tuscaloosa, Alabama. I recalled how the fellowship as equals with black faculty and staff had enriched and stretched my attitudes.

Then I thought of the black minister friends that I had recently made in Anniston. Nimrod Reynolds, Bob McClain, and George Smitherman were trying to lead their people in breaking out of the shackles of segregation. I then thought of the two families whose houses had been shot into this very afternoon. Neither of the families had been active in civil rights. The shootings were random violence against blacks. They, like our family, were celebrating Mother's Day in the quietness of their homes. All at once there was the loud blast of a shotgun, followed by the shattering of glass. I could only imagine the look of fear on the little children's faces. I could feel the emotion of a father who was helpless to protect his wife and children from such dastardly and unwarrented acts.

And I thought, "To accept this role of Chairman is right. I do not know what will happen, but I am convinced this is the right thing to do, and I will leave the future in God's hands." I got up and walked into the rooms where my three children were sleeping and looked at them. Then I got back in the bed and finally went to sleep.

THINGS WERE HAPPENING in the black community that Sunday night. On Sunday nights meetings were regularly held at the Seventeenth Street Baptist Church. This night was an especially emotionally charged meeting. Word of the shooting into the black St. John's Methodist Church, and into the homes of two black families had spread rapidly through the black community. As the people gathered at the church this night, there were more guns, knives, and clubs than usual. Some men remained outside the church as guards.

Anniston's black citizens also knew that violence had been escalating in Birmingham. The night before, the Klan had bombed the Gaston Motel in an attempt to assassinate Martin Luther King, Jr. In Birmingham, blacks were saying, "If they bomb us, why can't we bomb them?" The Klan broke plate glass windows in the stores of downtown Birmingham merchants who were giving in to some of the black demands.

Claude Dear and Miller Sproull were wise to get word to Nimrod Reynolds and Bob McClain late Sunday afternoon that a biracial committee was definitely going to be appointed the coming week. With that knowledge the two ministers were able to restrain the angry and restless people for the present.

On Monday morning I met with Claude Dear and Miller Sproull. They indicated they were going to appoint five white men and four black men to what would be called a "Biracial Human Relations Council." Miller was going to pick the four other whites and Claude was going to pick four blacks. It would later often be said that the Council was composed of four whites and four blacks, and Phil Noble! Claude said he wanted to include Nimrod Reynolds and Bob McClain as they were leaders in the black community. They were the two ministers that had come to me earlier to express their concerns. It was not felt that it would be a problem to get blacks to serve on the Council, but getting whites willing to serve might be more difficult. A legal counsel would be appointed for the Council.

The acts on Mother's Day of shooting into a church and the homes of Negroes was the culmination of many cowardly acts by Ku Klux Klan members and other hoodlums, but this time it produced a strong reaction in the community.

The following editorial appeared in the *Anniston Star* on Monday, May 13th:

Seldom have the decent citizens of Anniston suffered such an

The Anniston City Commission, 1963: Miller Sproull, Claude Dear, Jack Suggs.

ignominious setback as the crime that took place here Sunday afternoon with the wanton shotgun firing on residences occupied by two Negro families and on St. John's Methodist Church in south Anniston. This paper on several occasions has stated that one of the greatest obligations of the white race in this state is to help the Negro race in its efforts to hold dignified worship in its churches and to build a larger and better Christian influence in the state, as elsewhere. But instead of trying to spread the spirit of Christianity and to bring about a better citizenship among the Negro race, the Ku Klux Klan or whoever else it was that committed the Sunday Mother's Day crime, needs to be given the full force of the law as punishment in this instance. We do not agree with Gov. Wallace that the President of the United States should keep hands off entirely in an outrage such as this Mother's Day crime. For in such an instance, we should not consider who enforces the law, but how the law is to be upheld. On the other hand, however, Mayor Claude Dear is to be commended for his offer to give a reward to any person who will give positive help in bringing to the bar of justice the mean men who

ruined the observance of Mother's Day in such an outrageous way as
that of yesterday."[23]

The City Commission met on Tuesday, May 14. Two letters urging
the formation of a biracial committee were read. One was from the
rector, wardens and vestry of Grace Episcopal Church, and the other was
from the Anniston Ministerial Association, which by then was composed
of black and white ministers. The First Presbyterian Church had voted to
send such a letter on Thursday, May 9, but the clerk did not mail the
letter until Wednesday, May 15, almost a week after the Session had
passed its recommendation. (Was it foot-dragging?) Commissioner
Sproull said the Chamber of Commerce had also requested the establishment of such a committee. The Chamber office denied that a resolution
had been adopted, though it was acknowledged that the Chamber's
general manager, Frank Akers, had made the request on behalf of the
Chamber Executive Committee.

The City Commission met again on Thursday and passed two
significant resolutions. The minutes for May 16, 1963, include Resolution Number 3152 which reads:

> BE IT RESOLVED by the Board of Commissioners of the City of
> Anniston, Alabama, as follows: Section 1. That the Human Relations
> Council of the City of Anniston, is hereby created. Section 2. The duties
> and responsibilities of the Human Relations Council shall be to make
> recommendations to the Board of Commissioners of the City of Anniston,
> Alabama, concerning human relations in this community. But the
> Human Relations Council shall not interfere with the operation of
> private business. Section 3. The Human Relations Council shall be
> composed of nine members to be named by the Board of Commission-
> ers of the City of Anniston, Alabama, and the term of office for
> membership on the Human Relations Council shall be one year. Section
> 4. The Chairman of the Human Relations Council shall be named by
> the Board of Commissioners from the membership of the Council.
> Section 5. The Board of Commissioners shall appoint a legal counsel

who will attend meetings of the Human Relations Council. Section 6. The members of the Human Relations Council shall be citizens of the City of Anniston without outside influence which would conflict with local interest. Section 7. The members of the Human Relations Council shall serve without compensation. Section 8. The Human Relations Council shall meet in a regular meeting once a month at a time and place to be agreed upon by the Council. Special meetings can be called by the Chairman. Section 9. This resolution shall become effective immediately upon its passage and adoption. Passed and adopted this 16th day of May, 1963.[24]

At the same May 16th meeting of the City Commission, Resolution No. 3153 was adopted:

BE IT RESOLVED by the Board of Commissioners of the City of Anniston, Alabama, as follows: Section 1. That the following citizens of the City of Anniston, Alabama, are hereby appointed to the Human Relations Council of the City of Anniston, Alabama:
  1. J. Phillips Noble, who shall serve as Chairman
  2. Marcus A. Howze
  3. William B. McClain
  4. Grant Oden
  5. Leonard Roberts
  6. N. Quintus Reynolds
  7. Fred Vann
  8. Wilfred Galbraith
  9. Raleigh Byrd
Section 2. The attorney for the Human Relations Council shall be Roy M. Woolf, who shall serve without compensation. Passed and adopted this 16th day of May 1963.[25]

Fred Vann called me the day he had agreed to serve on the Council. He was the business agent for Local 151 Union and was thought by Miller Sproull to be a good representative of a large segment of the

ORIGINAL MEMBERS OF THE HUMAN RELATIONS COUNCIL

Top: Wilfred Galbraith, Edwin Cosper, N. Q. Reynolds. Center: Raleigh Byrd, Leonard Roberts, Phil Noble. Bottom: William B. McClain, Marcus A. Howze. Not pictured: Grant Oden.

population. Fred Vann wanted to know what we expected the Council to do and how we would proceed. I explained to him that the Council would be a place where responsible white and black representatives of the community could meet and hear the concerns of each and engage in negotiations that hopefully would help Anniston handle its racial problems in a peaceful way. He expressed some reservation about being on the Council, but said he had participated in many negotiations in his union. In a couple of days when the names of the Council members appeared in the newspaper, he called me back and was very angry. He indicated he would in no way be part of a Council designed to "sell out to the niggers." Apparently someone had gotten to him and caused him to be afraid to serve. He resigned and Harold Edwin Cosper was named in his place.

President John F. Kennedy wrote a letter to Mayor Dear on May 17, which was read by Miller Sproull to the May 23 meeting of the City Commission.

The letter commended the Anniston city commission for establishing the Human Relations Council. Kennedy indicated the action appointing the Council "is a sensible one and one that should serve as a guide and model for other communities throughout the Unites States." Mayor Claude Dear would later say that he heard from many, maybe as many as one hundred, towns and communities who wanted information about how Anniston had set up the Council and what results it was getting.

The *Anniston Star* announced the appointment of the Human Relations Council with my picture and that of a white member, Marcus Howze. The announcement indicated that the resolutions creating the Human Relations Council and appointing its members were adopted by two to one votes. It said that a "grim-faced Jack Suggs voted no on each proposal." In announcing the city commission's actions it also pointed out that the resolution said clearly "the purpose of the group should be to make 'recommendations concerning human relations' and that its members were to be 'without outside influence.'" As if to point up that all the members of the Human Relations Council were *local* persons, it identified each and their role in the community as follows:

The Rev. Mr. Noble is pastor of the First Presbyterian Church and President of the Anniston Ministerial Association.

The Rev. Mr. Reynolds, a native of Five Points in Chambers County, is pastor of the Seventeenth Street Baptist Church. Both [McClain and Reynolds] are graduates of Clark College in Atlanta. The Rev. Mr. McClain is also a graduate of Boston College. The Rev. Mr. Reynolds attended Gammon Theological Seminary in Atlanta.

Byrd is the operator of Byrd Cleaners in South Anniston. He has been active in the Southside Progressive Club.

Oden, an employee at Fort McClellan, is a member of Mt. Zion Baptist Church and has been active in the Anniston-Calhoun County Voters League.

Galbraith is executive editor of the *Anniston Star*.

Vann is business agent for Painters Local 151.

Howze is president of the Commercial National Bank and a former president of the Anniston Chamber of Commerce.

Roberts, an active member of the Chamber's industrial development committee, is president of Classe Ribbon Company, and a vice president of Adelaide Mills and Tape-Craft, Inc.[26]

When the City Commission appointed the biracial Human Relations Council, Mayor Dear was very much aware of the probable response of Kenneth Adams and his Klan followers. For years Adams had owned a filling station on the west side of Anniston on Highway 202. Large signs at the station proclaimed "Whites Only." Having grown up on the west side of town, Mayor Dear said he knew Adams and many of his followers very well. Claude reported that on the day the appointment of the Council was announced, he purposefully drove out to Adams's filling station. Kenneth and several of his "boys" were there. Claude said he got a bottle of Coke out of the drink machine, and stood talking to Kenneth Adams. He knew that Adams was aware the Council had been appointed. Claude said the subject did not come up, but he had wanted his presence that day to say, "Yes, I have appointed the Council and I am not afraid of you." Of course, Claude also said he very carefully kept the Coke bottle in his hand until he got back into his car in case he needed to use it. He reported strong angry stares on the part of Adams and his "boys," but no untoward action.

The *Anniston Star* account of the appointment of the council gave some recent historical perspective on what lay behind the action of the City Council:

> The formation of the bi-racial group has received strong support from two groups—churchmen and merchants. The Anniston Ministerial Association adopted a resolution asking [for] such a committee this week, and has in fact been working quietly for several months to bring its organization about. The officials of Grace Episcopal Church indicated they favored the move Monday, the day after the Rev. Alvin S. Bullen urged its support in a Sunday morning sermon. The Rev. Mr. Noble also asked his congregation to support the committee. Both sermons were delivered on the second anniversary of the Mother's Day burning of a bus loaded with Freedom Riders here. The move for formation of the committee gained in intensity after bloody and destructive Saturday night riots in Birmingham and the firing of shotgun blasts into two Negro homes and a church here. However, the formation of the committee has been advocated here for some time. Dr. Gordon A. Rodgers, a Negro candidate [for City Commissioner]in last summer's elections, used the idea as a main plank in his platform. Miller Sproull, Anniston's finance commissioner, advocated the committee in his campaign, and informed sources say he has strongly favored its early establishment. Authoritative sources have described Mayor Claude Dear as probably favorably inclined toward establishing the committee for some time, but is somewhat hesitant because of its political implications. Many Anniston businessmen and industrialists have favored the bi-racial committee as a possible way to prevent racial discord in the city. They figure the job of selling prospective industrialists on Anniston is almost impossible with the spectre of racial clashes hanging over the city like the acrid smoke from a dynamite blast.[27]

The same day the council was announced in the newspaper there was a strongly supportive editorial pointing out that President Kennedy had recently said "the best way to avoid racial violence is to open lines of communication between local spokesmen for both races." The editorial said this was exactly what the Anniston city fathers were trying to do. The editorial bluntly said,

> . . . candor compels the admission that the setting up of a bi-racial council locally might incur the displeasure of Governor George Wallace and his "body-in-the-school-door" nonsense. He might try purse-strings tightening by way of reprisal. But the risk that we take in this regard is nothing like the risk involved in trying to ignore racial discontent. Indeed, on the basis of his pledge time and again to uphold law and order, Wallace himself is in effect, on the side of those who would establish communications between the races. [28]

The reaction to the Mother's Day violence on the part of the police was swift. Police Commissioner Jack Suggs, although he had voted against the appointment of the Human Relations Council, made it clear that he intended to enforce the law and would tolerate no violence by blacks or whites. This is one of the elements that enabled the Human Relations Council to be effective in its work. A May 20 newspaper article written by my good friend, Cody Hall, the *Anniston Star* editor, gives a more detailed description of the violence and potential violence in Anniston. There were big headlines on the front page:

ADAMS BOOKED IN SHOOTING INCIDENT
SUGGS REVEALS CHARGES FILED AGAINST TWO MEN
    Police Commissioner L. S. (Jack) Suggs announced this afternoon the arrest of local oil dealer Kenneth Adams in connection with shotgun blasts fired at two Negro homes May 12.
    Booked in a companion case was William H. Boyd, Jr. Both were expected to make bond shortly after lunch.
    Det. Capt. C. F. Pate said Adams was booked on two charges of

"firing a shotgun into or against a dwelling house" on warrants signed by the occupants, Jesse Clark and Tom Dokes.

Boyd was booked on charges of assault with a gun filed by Jessie Mae Jemison and Ada Bell Ross and Adams was charged with disorderly conduct by the same women. The latter charges stem from an incident on the same Mother's Day afternoon, Pate said.

The women complained they were driving along Hwy. 202 (the Birmingham Highway) when Adams and Boyd, with two other men in the car, pulled their car over to the side of the highway. Boyd pulled out a pistol and fired it over their automobile. Pate said the women reported, and Adams ordered them to turn around and head the other way.

The women said they had their children with them in the car at the time of the incident, the officer noted.

Shotgun-firing charges against Adams, Pate said, result from the occasion a week ago yesterday when two residences and the St. John's Methodist Church, all in South Anniston, were struck by shot.

At that time, witnesses said the shooting was done by four white men in a 1958 model Chevrolet bearing a dealer's tag. No one was wounded by the shot. One of the blasts struck the side of the church. Another shattered a window of the Clark house.

Pate said the two other men in the car when the two women were stopped on Hwy. 202 have not been identified.

Boyd was identified in a line-up of five persons by the two witnesses, the captain said. Boyd, age 22, is a resident of Anniston, Route 1. Adams, age 43, is a local resident.

Comm. Suggs cited the officers involved in the arrests for long hours put in on the investigation and praised them for their diligent work.

The shooting here May 12 followed by only a few hours rioting in Birmingham that resulted in an order from President Kennedy sending riot-trained troops into Fort McClellan and Maxwell Air Force Base.

Adams was booked two years ago in another Mother's Day incident—the burning on Hwy. 202 at Forsyth's Store of a Greyhound bus bearing a group of Freedom Riders.

He came to trial with several others in the case but was freed on a directed verdict of acquittal by the judge.

In 1956 he was charged with another group in attacking Negro singer Nat (King) Cole on the stage of the Municipal Auditorium in Birmingham.

Indicted on a felony charge of assault with intent to murder in that case, he pleaded guilty to a reduced count and was fined $50 and costs.

The May 12 incidents broke the expected calm of a Sunday afternoon here.

Members of the Dokes family at 321 S. Christine Avenue and the Clark family at 301 S. Christine Avenue were at home when the shotgun blasts were directed at their residences.

Mayor Claude Dear immediately offered a $500 reward for information leading to the arrest and conviction of the man involved and another $500 was added to that by the Chamber of Commerce.

Hours after the shooting incident, trucks began rolling through Anniston bearing the Kennedy-dispatched troops to Fort McClellan where they are still bivouacked.[29]

The image Anniston had of Fort McClellan in the early 1960s was of a peacetime facility. Military personnel came and went and did not have a great deal of interaction with the average Anniston citizen. We all knew the base was there, but Fort McClellan had its structure and way of life and Anniston had its way of life. Annistonians were used to the coming and going of army vehicles. But now truck loads of troops were moving through the streets of Anniston to Fort McClellan with a designated purpose. If things got out of hand in Anniston or Birmingham, the troops would be put into action. This was viewed as good and bad. Good, in the sense that control would be exercised over a situation that could tear a community apart through rioting and violence. Bad, in the sense that Anniston might be put under martial law.

This was an entirely new reality for most Annistonians. Heretofore Fort McClellan was a strong, quiet asset to the Anniston community. It added millions of dollars annually to the city economy. The Chamber of Commerce and the entire business community cultivated good relations with the Army's top brass and other personnel. In addition to being a training base for regular troops, Fort McClellan was also the headquarters for the Women's Army Corps (WACS) and the army's Chemical School.

One small aspect of Anniston's relation to Fort McClellan was that it offered good hunting to those interested in that activity. During hunting season when there were no army maneuvers scheduled, hunting was allowed on the Fort's extensive acres. A permit would have to be secured and a map would be given to the hunters with the areas clearly specified where hunting was allowed and where it was strictly prohibited. I do not know to what extent the general public could obtain hunting permits, but city officials and a number of business people that I knew could obtain the permits. I never hunted there except as a guest of a friend who could readily get permits. One day, Henry (Red) Smith, a local businessman and a member of First Presbyterian Church, took me to Fort McClellan to hunt quail. He was a personal friend of the Commanding Officer, who had given him a pass with privileges to hunt any time during the hunting season, except when there were maneuvers. We took two of his bird dogs and my Esau and Jacob, who were given to me as three-month-old pointer puppies by my brother, C. R. (Dudy) Noble, who was then athletic director at Mississippi State University (the MSU baseball stadium bears his name). Since they were from the same litter, I decided to name them Esau and Jacob after two brothers in the Old Testament of the Bible. Esau in the Bible was described as "hairy all over" and as one who loved to hunt. Jacob was sly and cunning and often outsmarted his brother. It turned out that the dog Esau loved to hunt, always running with his head high and tail wagging. Jacob, on the other hand, slipped around rather slyly and was far less energetic, but he had the best nose and found more birds. I always enjoyed the reaction of new hunting companions to the dog's names. Baptists would nearly always know the Esau and Jacob story from the Bible. Presbyterians and Methodists usually would recognize that these were Biblical names even if they didn't know the particulars. Episcopalians, Catholics, and Unitarians would have no clue!

On this day Red and I were having a good hunt and had found a couple of coveys of quail. All at once two carloads of soldiers bore down on us with sirens blaring. Red identified himself with the pass from the commanding officer and indicated that he had hunted many times at Fort McClellan. The soldiers replied that we were hunting in a highly restricted area. There were several old, apparently vacant buildings a few hundred yards from us. They must have had some significance to making the area restricted. The soldiers said to Red, "You all haven't been hunting close to those buildings, have you?" Now, we had not only been hunting close to the buildings, but I had shot a quail that had landed right on the apex of one of the buildings. We had shot at the dead bird once to try to get it to fall off the roof. Then "Red" had driven his pick-up truck to the side of the building thinking we might get from the truck to the rather low eave of the building and then crawl up the roof and get the bird. But to the soldiers' query as to whether or not we had been hunting close to the buildings, "Red" had quickly replied, "Oh, no, we haven't been hunting near them." At that moment he locked his eyes on me, and I could see that he suddenly was thinking, "Here I am hunting with my preacher and I have just told a big lie!" He quickly amended his response to the soldiers by saying, "Well, yeah. We have been pretty close to them." We both laughed about this considerably, but not before the soldiers had taken us into headquarters to the officer in charge of such infractions of the rules, and let us sit and wait for an hour, before telling us we could go but were not to be found again hunting in a restricted area.

So with the army trucks rolling into Fort McClellan carrying soldiers that had been dispatched there by President Kennedy, to be used to quell riots in Birmingham or Anniston if any developed in the volatile situation, the Fort was seen in an additional relationship to Anniston to that of an economic asset and a happy hunting ground. It was clear to the Anniston community that with the close proximity of the Fort, any major racial disturbance could and would be responded to quickly.

My personal feeling about the availability of army troops was comparable to my feelings about the FBI. I felt it was a kind of security for those of us who were trying to work through the turbulent racial situations. Some help would come in for us if it were really needed. That feeling on my part may have been an illusion. The hymn says, "Safe and secure from all alarms." Hardly! But if serious "alarms" did come, a strong arm of help was nearby. Fortunately, we never had the need for activation of troops in the city of Anniston.

THE REACTION OF THE COMMUNITY to the appointment of the Human Relations Council also came quickly. Much of it was favorable, but it stirred opposition also. Despite Police Commissioner Suggs's pledge to enforce the law, there remained some question as to whether the policemen under him could be counted on, especially since Suggs had voted against the appointment of the Council. Miller Sproull, as Finance Commissioner, asked Suggs if he would call the policemen together and let him talk to them. Suggs agreed and Miller spoke to the group about the Christian duty to our fellowman; he even read some Bible verses to the officers. I believe this gathering had a good effect in encouraging the keeping of law and order without regard to race.

Sure enough, Governor George Wallace called Mayor Dear soon after receiving word of the appointment of the Human Relations Council. Wallace expressed his dislike of the Council's creation. The city was scheduled to get money from the State for its streets and roads. Also according to the Mayor, there were other funds controlled by the Governor that had been promised to the city. Wallace made a veiled threat to Mayor Dear, suggesting that future funds may not be available to Anniston. Mayor Dear replied to Governor Wallace that he had been speaking all across the nation about how the Federal Government had no business interfering in State affairs. "Now", he said, "are you going to come trying to interfere with the city of Anniston running its affairs? I am the elected Mayor and I will run the city the way I think best." When the conversation was finished, Mayor Dear called Senator A. C. Shelton of Calhoun County and told him of his conversation with Wallace. Shelton called the Governor and within an hour, according to Mayor Dear, the Governor's office called him to find out what funds he needed for the city's streets and roads, and promised they would be forthcoming.[30]

The attention of the President of the United States to the appointing of a Human Relations Council in Anniston at a time when Birmingham was in the throes of a real civil rights crisis points up the significance of the city's action. We did not fully realize it at the time, but this was a highly significant historical event, not just for Anniston, but for the civil rights movement in the South. One city was showing other stressed cities that there was a way, apart from violence, to work through difficult racial problems. Many other cities had not been brave enough or wise enough to appoint biracial committees. At the time, Anniston uniquely made a huge contribution toward solving the racial troubles of the 1960s.

ON MAY 22, the *Anniston Star*, which constantly gave positive support to the appointing of the Council and to its work when it got started, had an editorial by publisher Harry Brandt Ayers with the heading: Kennedy, Aide Praise City Commission Act; Local Visit is Hinted. Washington Attorney General Robert Kennedy and his chief civil rights aide Tuesday hailed Anniston city officials for opening lines of communication between the races there. The editorial in part was as follows:

> In an exclusive interview, Kennedy and Assistant Attorney General Burke Marshall called creation of the Human Relations Council "foresighted" and "in the best traditions of the country." At the same time, it was learned from a source close to the Attorney General that the President's younger brother would like to visit Anniston. The sources disclosed that Kennedy would accept an invitation to visit the model city, but emphasized that the purpose of the trip "wouldn't be to preach." He said the Attorney General would like to come to the northeast Alabama city to meet local citizens and officials and for "a mutual exchange of views." Kennedy and his top civil rights troubleshooter talked to this *Star* reporter in the Attorney General's spacious office. They emphasized that cautious action put the initiative to handle racial problems in the hands of local leaders and would discourage outsiders of both races from taking command. "The important thing is

that the local people, at the local level, are trying to solve their problems," asserted the Attorney General. He declared "the action taken by the Anniston City Commission is in the best traditions of this country." Marshall, whose mild but penetrating mediation halted Birmingham demonstrations and arranged the truce agreement, called the action "foresighted." He asserted, "I think the experience of Birmingham shows that a crises of that kind can be avoided by starting the line of communication on the local level." Marshall said the dialogue should rightly begin between local leaders of both races, asserting "you can underscore my feeling that it shouldn't take place between outsiders." The Assistant Attorney General, whose restrained and understanding mediation has gained the confidence of both races, said experiences throughout the nation led him to believe that Anniston's approach was the right one. Kennedy pointed out that communication was essential, not only to solve the South's problems but that it is equally pertinent to cities like Chicago, Boston and Englewood, N.J. The Chief Federal law enforcement officer, who is acutely aware of his bad image in the south, was at first hesitant about commenting on Anniston's action. One foot in the drawer of his desk, the sleeves of his rumpled blue shirt rolled up, the younger Kennedy grinned boyishly and observed, "I don't know whether a comment from me would be appreciated."[31]

Mayor Dear confirmed that there had been talk that Bobby Kennedy might come to Anniston to talk with him. When Mr. E. D. (Sonny) King, Jr., who owned the King Motor Company and also was president of the Anniston National Bank learned that Bobby Kennedy might come to Anniston, he sent Kennedy an invitation. He offered to "hold a cocktail party" for the Attorney General should he come. It was probably fortunate for Sonny King that he did not come—a welcoming cocktail party for Bobby Kennedy in Anniston, Alabama, indeed!

However, while Bobby Kennedy did not come to Anniston, soon after the appointment of the Council two top RFK aides did come to talk to Mayor Dear. They wanted copies of the resolutions establishing the Council. Mayor Dear indicated that they distributed that material to many cities, towns and communities. He estimated that it had an influence on a hundred or more communities as they sought to deal with racial issues.

On May 27, the *Anniston Star* ran an editorial citing the fact that the *New York Herald Tribune* had an editorial entitled "Anniston Shows the Way." The article was as follows:

> "Amid all the other news, from Alabama comes one small, cheering item. Seems that two Negro homes and a Negro church in Anniston, Alabama were peppered by shotgun blasts not long ago. Law-enforcement officials moved in promptly and arrested a suspect (a former Ku Klux Klansman). But that wasn't all. The city, on its own initiative, also set up a bi-racial Human Relations Commission.
>
> "Mayor Claude Dear received a letter about it this week from President Kennedy, praising the commission's establishment as 'a model for other communities throughout the U.S.,' which it ought to be. In making a co-operative community effort to solve racial problems on a community level, and to do so in time, the Alabama city of Anniston is calmly and sensibly meeting the future—and making it brighter."
>
> The foregoing is noteworthy by reason of its commendation of positive steps that are being taken in our part of the country in the interest of racial harmony. This sort of comment appears infrequently in the Northern metropolitan press, and for this reason, we are all the more grateful to the Herald Tribune.[32]

The Session of the First Presbyterian Church wrote a letter to the Anniston City Commission thanking it for creating the Human Relations Council.

But not all response was favorable. A letter to the editor of the *Anniston Star* from Paul Marler may have expressed the views of many people who were not in favor of the appointment of the Council. It said:

> I deplore the recent action by the Anniston City Commission and question the legality of such acts in creating a Race Relations Board, or

whatever you may call it. What power does the Commission have to create such a board? and who will pay the attorney's fees? When and why will this attorney be needed to represent this Board? I also deplore all those persons connected with getting the Commission of Anniston involved in such a thing as this. If these so-called do-gooders want to create such a board, then let them do so; but this is not—and should not—be the function of the City of Anniston, Alabama. This Board has no legal status, and any and all action, or arguments to it, or caused by it, will only be a reflection on the name of Anniston, Alabama which all interested citizens are trying to keep clean in this respect. When a Negro or white person or persons have a problem to discuss with the Commission, the chambers of these commissioners are always open to any and all citizens, regardless of their race. Also, the commissioners will listen to any recommendation from any Board, or committee, on any matter, and act as it sees fit, as it has always done. Therefore, I respectfully ask that the Anniston Commission attend to their duly-appointed duties and leave racial matters to colored people of this city. White and Negro law breakers will be caught and punished for unlawful acts, and harmony will prevail among the white and colored people of Anniston. We do not need any kind of board, or outside agitators, or local headline hunters, to tell us how to get along with each other.[33]

I did not know what kind of reaction to expect to me personally. For the most part there was eerie silence from my parishioners and friends. At the first meeting of the Session (the local governing body) of the First Presbyterian Church, I reported officially what they already knew: that I had accepted the appointment of the city to be the chairman of the biracial Human Relations Council. There was only deafening silence from the Session members. From time to time a church member or even an elder of the Church would make a sarcastic comment such as, "So you and Miller Sproull are going to solve the nigger problem?"

Good support came from my associate minister, the Rev. John Rhea Hall, as well as from the Rev. James Lowry, a young minister of the Good Shepherd Presbyterian Church in the east Anniston area called Golden

Springs. First Presbyterian had begun the development of this new church. The wife of one of my fellow Presbyterian ministers called and said, "You are the man of the hour. The whole city and community is waiting to see what you can do. We are praying for you." I was glad to know she and others were praying for me, but I already felt enough pressure without her telling me that the whole community had their eyes on me to see what I could do!

A few church members gave me strong support. No one could have been more supportive than Mary Catherine White, who had been the church secretary for many years. She and I had often discussed race relations in general, and more specifically in the South and in Anniston. Her strong Christian faith had led her to basically the same conclusions I had reached regarding race. She took a certain pride in my upcoming role as chairman of the Human Relations Council.

Tweed Johnson was the Youth Director at the YMCA. He and I used to quail hunt with my dogs, Esau and Jacob. He found it difficult to believe that I was willing to be the chairman of the Council. His reaction was one of mingled pride, fear, and awe. He and his wife, Kathleen, had long since had their view of race relations effected by their warm Christian faith. Gilbert and Florence Steil were strong Christians who had recently come to Anniston from Patterson, New Jersey. He was one of the executives at the Linen Thread Company in Blue Mountain, a community adjoining Anniston. Their support was not loud or vocal, but it was strong and solid. Lena Smith and Jean Talley had grown up in Livingston, Alabama, in the heavy atmosphere of segregation. No two people could have been more loyal and supportive to my family and me. There were many others who remained loyal friends, though not necessarily supportive of my activity regarding race relations.

A few members, including those named above, began meeting in our homes on Sunday nights for small group Bible study. This group gave Betty and me the good support that we so desperately needed.

With the establishment of the bi-racial Human Relations Council, action had been officially taken that gave Anniston, both black and white, hope that a way could be found through its troubled waters.

8

Getting Started

WHEN THE HUMAN RELATIONS COUNCIL was appointed, the Mayor, perhaps being more aware of the danger than we were, gave us advice. He said, "Do not announce your meetings. You as chairman call the members an hour before the meeting time and tell them where the meeting will be. That way, you will decrease the risk that you will be bombed." We took his advice. For several months, we did not meet at a regular time or place. At each meeting we would set the date and time of the next meeting, and then a half-hour or an hour before the meeting, I would call and tell council members the place. We did not meet in the same place each time. We met in the YMCA Building, the First Presbyterian Church, the board room of a bank, the Chamber of Commerce building, and other places. In the early days, it was very rare for any of the members to miss a meeting, such was the sense of importance of what we were trying to do and the depth of commitment made by each member.

I had known previously all of the white members except one, and I knew two of the four black members. Basically the white and black members were strangers to each other. As we began to get to know each other, I talked to the group about our need to have respect for each other and to develop a sense of trust in each other.

There were several interesting ironies along the way. In our ministerial meetings where black and white ministers had been meeting together for some time, we had developed such relationships that we called each other by first names. Of course, the custom in the South had been that blacks were always called by first names and were never addressed as Mr. or Mrs. Newspapers never referred to blacks by Mr. or Mrs. The minister at Grace Episcopal Church told one of his members who was to serve later on the Human Relations Council that we had gotten to a first-name basis, black and white. The member was indignant that there would be such familiarity that blacks would call whites by their first names. It was interesting to hear the white members of the Council very carefully addressing the black members as Mr., which in the segregated society, had not been done previously.

Little such things of symbolic importance were a part of our getting acquainted with each other. Bob McClain, minister of Haven Chapel Methodist Church, took some time to talk to us about the pronunciation of the word, Negro. Most, if not all of the whites, had long since pronounced it "Negra." Bob said it should be pronounced like "knee" and "grow." Some were a bit irritated by such a pronunciation lesson, but it was important for Bob and the other black members to make that clear. It was a symbol of respect. All the white members became very careful to pronounce Negro correctly and to address the black members as Mister. Of course, black people had always used Mister when addressing white people.

Early on the black members presented a list of their concerns. The list ran the gamut from the patterns of segregation that affected their everyday lives to discrimination in jobs. With regard to job discrimination, blacks were confined primarily to menial jobs. None clerked in stores, nor worked in offices. There were no black firemen or policemen. Another concern was that the so-called public facilities were not available to blacks, such as the library, swimming pools, or golf courses. City parks were segregated. Public transportation required segregation with blacks only sitting in the back, if there was room. The waiting rooms in bus and train stations were segregated. Theaters were segregated, with only the balcony for blacks. Public restaurants were not available to them. Soda fountains in drug stores and lunch counters were unavailable for their use. Where there were public restrooms and water fountains, they were marked "white" and "colored." The unions in the factories were segregated. Getting justice in the courts was another concern. Crimes by blacks against whites were dealt with severely while whites were seldom punished for crimes against blacks. Another concern was strictly segregated churches. Whereas whites had always been welcome at black churches, blacks were never welcome at white churches. The only exception being a maid or a servant who attended the funeral of a white member of the family.

Segregation was strict and severe, and every day blacks faced its dehumanizing effect. In the early stages of our work, one of the strongest and most influential white members, Leonard Roberts, said, "I have no intention of being a part of dismantling the pattern of segregation which has been a part of our southern way of life for many years." It was exactly my intention to do just that!

As time went on, it was interesting to see the growth that occurred, especially the attitudes of the white members. Leonard Roberts, who had said he did not want to dismantle the South's segregation system, had a son in the military. He told me of visiting his son on his military base. While at a cocktail reception his son said, "Dad, I want you to meet a friend of mine." The father said that before he turned to see his son's friend, he knew he was going to be black! This was part of this Human Relations Council member's growing experience that contributed to change in attitudes. Good healthy experiences of interchange between blacks and whites were happening all over.

While the black members of the Council presented the long list of their concerns, they did not "demand" immediate action by the Council. They had come to serve on the Council with hopes that they had found a forum where their concerns ultimately would be addressed. They never voiced the threat that if certain things were not done, there would be demonstrations and/or boycotts. However, all members of the Council were keenly aware of the probability of such action unless reasonable progress was made. "How little can we give and still keep demonstrations and boycotts from happening" might best summarize the attitude of the white members of the Council.

The Council looked carefully at the list its black members had presented and began with what was considered the simplest and easiest things to do. The decision was made to begin with the white and colored signs over drinking fountains and rest rooms in public places. The first group of people who were willing to meet with us were the managers of the "dime" stores, Kress, Roses and Silvers, that were local branches of national retailing chains. Their national management officers instructed the managers of the local stores to meet with us. At the first meeting with these managers, the three agreed to take down the white and colored signs and we agreed not to announce or draw public attention to this action. It would be quietly done. The three managers came back to our next meeting to report to us what they had done. They all reported that the signs had been removed without incident. One of them noted that he had thought it was going to be difficult to remove the signs as they were in marble, but when they examined it, they realized that the words "white" and "colored" were on a small piece of marble that could be easily slid out of the wall mounting of marble. I remember saying, "Maybe this can be a symbol to us. What we think will be very difficult may not be as difficult as we think." I am not sure our task worked out just that way, but at least that early result symbolized a hope that we could get our task done, and, hopefully, without violence.

Sit-ins at lunch counters were happening in North Carolina and sit-ins were rapidly spreading across the South. We encouraged the managers of the dime stores to be willing to desegregate their lunch counters. They instructed their employees to serve black customers if they came. They came and were served for the most part without violent incidents occurring.

As our work progressed, I was always aware of the need for a sensitive and delicate balance between what the black community wanted and what the white community was willing to give, if violence was to be avoided. Enough progress needed to be made so that the black community could see and feel the progress, but slow enough so that the white community would not "dig in their heels" against any progress. One day a white member of the Council said to me privately, "Phil, you remind me of a baseball pitcher that does a big wind-up on the pitcher's mound as if he is going to throw a burning pitch, and then he just lobs the ball over the home plate!" Perhaps that was a correct image of what we were doing to create and preserve a fragile climate in which we eventually could solve our problems without the violent eruptions that were happening all over the South. There was general support in the black community and a good measure of support in the white community. While there was criticism of what we were trying to do, some good support developed. Some white supporters of our effort suggested that they form an organization with an acronym that indicated support for our efforts. I discouraged it, fearing such action might polarize the community.

During this time I began to receive more telephone calls during the night, often around midnight. They were always derogatory and often threatening. Occasionally when my wife, Betty, would answer the telephone, on Saturday night, a gravelly voice would say, "Let me speak to that black ape." When she replied, "You have the wrong number," the caller would say, "Naw, I don't have the wrong number. Let me speak to that black ape."

One night Betty woke in the middle of the night seeing light streaming in the front bedroom windows and reflecting on the ceiling. Thinking it was the flickering light from a cross burning in the front yard, she rushed into the two bedrooms where our three children were sleeping to shut the doors lest they see what was happening. When she returned to the bedroom and looked out the front window there was no cross burning. Someone may have been shining lights or it may have been her dreams or imagination, but this incident reveals how tense we all were during these times.

I began to sleep with a baseball bat under my bed. I do not know how it would have helped if the house had been bombed or if I had been attacked, but it did give me some measure of psychological comfort. A bit later I slept with my shotgun with which I hunted, under the bed. Added comfort was given when I started keeping it loaded under my bed!

Almost every morning when I went to the car to take my children to school, I looked the car over carefully and raised the hood to try to see whether or not a bomb had been planted in it. Bob and Nimrod were getting daily telephone calls and written messages with warnings and death threats.

During this time we were constructing a new church building at the First Presbyterian Church. The FBI informed us that there had been bomb threats to our church. The Session discussed the matter, increased the insurance on the church, and also voted to hire a night guard at the church.

Often during this period, police were scheduled to circle all night between the Mayor's house, Miller Sproull's house and my house. In retrospect, we were amused by the story that Miller, being told that someone was going to bomb his house "that night," called his wife, Barbara, and told her not to worry, that he did not think that would happen and that he had to be in Atlanta that night for a meeting. But he doubled the insurance on his house!

Anonymous letters were received from time to time. While such letters were an irritant, they were not taken too seriously. I remembered a story about Phillips Brooks, the famous abolitionist Boston preacher. One Sunday he held up a sheet of paper in his pulpit that had only the word "fool" written on it. Then he said to his congregation that he had often had letters from persons who "forgot" to sign their name, but he had never had one where the writer had signed his name, but forgot to write the letter!

During this period and the months to follow, the KKK was active and it was never known just what they were going to do next. As it became obvious that Anniston was moving toward breaking down some of the segregation barriers, people like Connie Lynch and J. B. Stoner spoke in Anniston. They "hated blacks and Jews so much that they became evangelists of violence, traveling the South delivering fanatical racist speeches to whoever would listen," according to *Free at Last*.[34]

I later learned that my safety was a bit more tenuous than I had realized at the time. Brandt Ayers of the *Anniston Star,* with tongue in cheek, said he was a bit miffed because I was number one on the KKK hit list and he was only number two! Later, a lawyer in Anniston told me that when one of the KKK members tried to engage him to represent him in court, he revealed that he had often sat with a group who plotted how to kill Phil Noble and Miller Sproull. While I knew violence was possible and I was scared enough as it was, I am glad I did not know those two specific bits of information at the time.

But we did not escape completely all violence in our efforts. It occurred almost four months to the day after the appointment of the Human Relations Council when the public library was to be desegregated.

9

The Library "Incident"

SEPTEMBER 15, 1963, was blown into the history of the Civil Rights Movement. The world remembers that on that Sunday morning a dynamite bomb exploded in Birmingham's Sixteenth Street Baptist Church, and four laughing little black girls died. This terrible event overshadowed what happened later that afternoon in Anniston, when two black ministers of the gospel, a Baptist and a Methodist, were attacked by a mob of Klansmen and other hoodlums. The ministers' "offense" was in attempting to patronize the Anniston Public Library. While the Birmingham event shocked the nation, the Anniston event personalized the horrible violence of racial hatred for the Anniston community. These two events were explosions ignited by the collision of two cultures. One was a culture of freedom, privilege, and opportunity within which individuals could dream and aspire, limited only by his or her capabilities. The other was a culture of servitude and restriction, which put severe limitations on opportunities, regardless of individuals' potential capabilities. This combined cultural fabric was so deeply ingrained that any attempt to change it was sure to set off strong social conflict.

In Anniston in 1963, as elsewhere in the South, segregation was being seriously challenged, not just by a few leaders, but by a mass of previously oppressed people. As we have seen, leaders in Anniston, hoping to avoid the violence so often accompanying the collision of the two cultures in the South, had taken the wise and courageous step of appointing a biracial Human Relations Council. By September 1963, the Council had been at work for four months, maneuvering ever so carefully to bring change without provoking violence. Some few symbols of segregation had been removed, like "white" and "colored" drinking fountains and bathroom signs. A few lunch counters had been integrated. Many other concerns of the black community were being discussed. So far, so good. There had been many threats, but no further violence.

The Council recognized that as it was a city agency, appointed by the City Commission, the desegregation of city institutions should be the first priority. Even before appointment of the Council, Anniston's library board had discussed opening their facilities to the black community. Thus, the Carnegie Anniston Public Library seemed the most logical place to begin. The library facilities and their availability mirrored the school arrangement in the South: separate but presumably equal. They were separate all right, but never equal. This was the case in Anniston. On West Fourteenth Street there was a Carver Library, named after the famous Tuskegee Institute scientist. It was predictably small and resource-poor compared to the library facilities for whites. In the 1930s and 1940s, the Anniston Carnegie Library had a program for black school children who were brought in once a week on Thursdays and on the first Sunday of each month. Otherwise, Anniston blacks were allowed no use of their tax-supported central public library.

Conversations were held between the Human Relations Council and the library board and the library board voted to desegregate. While the City Commission never formally voted to approve the desegregation, Miller Sproull wrote Charlie Doster, chairman of the library board, stating, "This will assure you that if the Library Board elects to integrate the Anniston Public Library, it will have the support of a majority of the City Commission." He sent and signed the letter in his capacity as a commissioner.

As the Council considered how to effect the library desegregation, we decided that the first step would be for two black citizens to enter the Anniston Carnegie Library, quietly check out a book each, and leave

Anniston's Carnegie Public Library, 1963.

without lingering. The library staff would be prepared in advance to enroll the black patrons and to check out their chosen books. That would be it for that day.

The library board and the Human Relations Council then collaborated on a date when blacks would first use the library. Various dates and times were considered. All of this discussion and action was held in secret. We felt that if we announced the change the hard-core segregationists and violence-prone elements like the KKK would try to interfere, but if we just made the change quietly then trouble might be avoided.

In retrospect it appears that Sunday afternoon was not a good choice. We had hoped that blacks using the library would not be so noticeable at a time when people were spending a quiet Sunday afternoon with their families. This seemed logical to those of us participating in the discussions between the Council and the library board, because quiet Sunday afternoons with our families was the usual practice of most of us in the discussions, both black and white members. We did not take into account that Sunday, not being a work day, was a day when Klan members and others of like mind were free to pursue their activities. We had failed to realize that the Freedom Riders' bus burning was on a Sunday afternoon and that it was a Sunday when a church and several black homes in Anniston were fired into, which event had caused the City Commission to appoint the Human Relations Council in the first place. Other sporadic racial violence had also occurred on Sundays. Perhaps we were lulled by the fact that the small steps that had been taken by the Council up to that point had not produced a violent reaction. In any case, we had made our plan and we all expected the desegregation of the library to proceed smoothly. We had not anticipated that our plans would be leaked to the Klan.

The question of who the black pioneers would be had been an easy one. The black members of the Human Relations Council were leading the way for desegregation, they were committed to the process, and they were the logical ones for this assignment. Nimrod Reynolds and Bob McClain volunteered without hesitation. One was Baptist, the other Methodist. They were the two men who had come to see me some months before to initiate a dialogue about racial reconciliation and both had become my friends.

So, according to the prearranged plan, about 2 p.m. on Sunday, September 15, 1963, Nimrod and Bob parked their car on Tenth Street about half a block east of the library. As the two walked down the sidewalk in front of the library, a mob of fifty to a hundred whites who had been waiting in nearby parked cars and on the sidewalks surged forward. As Nimrod and Bob neared the steps, several men in the forefront of the mob jumped them. At least one attacker was wielding a length of chain and others had sticks, clubs, and guns. Nimrod was beaten to the sidewalk but managed to regain his feet and he and Bob sprinted back toward their car and jumped inside. However, the car had been blocked in by vehicles in front and behind. As they attempted to maneuver their car free, the mob surged around them. There was a sharp "splat" and the window on the driver's side shattered. Nimrod and Bob both said later that the noise was a shot and that the bullet broke the glass and passed directly behind their heads. They abandoned the car and managed to break through the mob and fled on foot. "If we'd stayed in the car, we would have been killed," Bob said afterwards. As they fled, the ministers were picked up by a passing motorist and taken to the emergency room at the Anniston Memorial Hospital.

The whole incident had taken only a few minutes yet they were terrifying minutes and underscored the ever-present potential for violence that the Council had tried so carefully to avoid. We were stunned by this development, not least because we thought the plan for Sunday afternoon had been secret. Nimrod and Bob had not told even their close friends Edward Wood and Ellis Grier of the plans. Wood and Grier were south of Anniston scouting out places to hunt when they heard the breaking news on their car radio. They hurried back to Anniston with their rifles. Edward told me later that it was fortunate that the violence had ended before he and Ellis got back because they would have been tempted to use their rifles to protect their ministers. Obviously, the ugly scene at the library could have been even worse than it was. The Anniston community was lucky no one was killed that day.[35]

I was called immediately by City Commissioner Miller Sproull. I said to Betty, who of course had known of the library plan, "Nimrod Reynolds and Bob McClain were just attacked by hoodlums as they went to the library this afternoon. They were beaten with sticks and chains."

"How badly were they hurt?" she replied.

"I do not know. Miller said that Claude Dear and Charlie Doster were getting ready to meet at his house now. He wants me to come. I will be back as soon as I can, but I do not know just when that will be." As I walked out of the door of the house, she pleaded with me to be careful. I of course said that I would, not really knowing what being careful meant in these circumstances.

Miller, Claude, Charlie, and I discussed the situation and Charlie thought we ought to call President Kennedy and alert him to the situation. We all were well aware that the racial situation in Birmingham had reached crisis proportions, even before the bombing of the Sixteenth

Street Baptist Church where the four girls were killed. What would happen now, no one knew. The black community in Anniston would already know what had happened in Birmingham. What had just happened to their minister leaders, Bob and Nimrod, would spread like wildfire through the community. The potential for explosive riots was great. Therefore a call was placed to President Kennedy, and we were told that the President would be landing in Washington within an hour and he would call back.

The four of us then went by police car to Nimrod's home. By now it was nighttime. When we arrived, the house was surrounded by a group of armed black men. They parted to let us through. We entered the house and were taken upstairs to the bedroom where Nimrod was on his bed, head bandaged. Bob was also in the room but did not appear to be physically hurt. Mrs. Reynolds seemed very distressed. We all expressed our concern for Nimrod and our outrage at what had happened. As I talked to Bob, he indicated that he had preached to a large crowd in Nimrod's Seventeenth Street Baptist Church that night. By this time

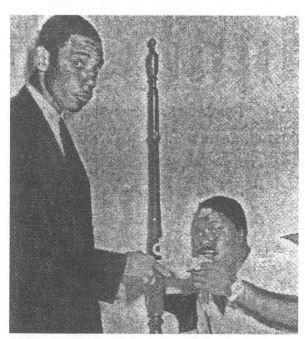

William (Bob) McClain visiting a bed-ridden N. Q. Reynolds after the two were attacked by a mob at the Anniston Public Library on September 15, 1963.

through our work together in the Ministerial Association and our work together on the Human Relations Council, I not only had a great deal of respect for Nimrod and Bob, but also a feeling of warm personal friendship, and I was deeply grieved about what they had just been through.

I said to Bob, "How could you preach tonight after what you and Nimrod went through this afternoon?" He looked directly at me and said, "Phil, the word of the Gospel had to be spoken tonight." I still get goose bumps when I think of the truth and power of that statement. Sensing how tense the people were, and how concerned they were for their pastor who was unable to be present because of injuries inflicted by the mob, Bob McClain called upon the congregation "not to hate," but to "clasp your hands around [your pastor] because he is right." In a sermon he preached years later, this is the way Bob McClain described his preaching that night:

> If I had any preaching ability at all, it was tested that evening at the mass meeting. It seemed the whole population of "colored people of Anniston, Alabama" turned out to seek some action against those who had assaulted and beaten us. Gathered at Seventeenth Street Church that Sunday evening at a mass meeting, twice or three times as many on the outside of the church as were inside of that over-crowded church, with speakers set up for the outside, it was my turn to try to quell the fever-pitched masses—some with their guns and other weapons in hand or nearby. Rev. Reynolds was still at the hospital [actually he was bandaged and in his bed at his house]—hurt too badly to be at the church—and I, with bruises and all, had to stand in that pulpit and preach non-violence and the message of the love of Jesus. Talk about preaching in a crisis! Talk about preaching dealing with the issues of life and death! I remember preaching from the text of Isaiah 53: ". . . He was wounded for our transgressions, he was bruised for our iniquities . . . He was oppressed, and he was afflicted, yet he opened not his mouth . . . the will of the Lord shall prosper in his hand." Somehow, by God's grace, we were able to save the bloodbath that would have surely come.[36]

Miller Sproull's residence, 1963, where President Kennedy called.

How fortunate we were that Christian ministers like Nimrod and Bob were at the forefront in leading their people in their efforts for freedom, justice and opportunity.

At Nimrod's home that evening, I had just finished leading those of us in the room in prayer when a policeman announced that President Kennedy was trying to return our call. The Mayor, Miller, Charlie and I jumped in the police car and were driven at high speed through town, back to Miller's house. Charlie talked to the President and related what had happened. As we have seen earlier, the President knew the city had appointed a bi-racial Human Relations Council and had commended Claude for its creation. Kennedy had even referred to it in a speech and cited it as a good approach to resolving racial problems. Now the President said he hoped things would settle down in Anniston and he expected that they would, but to keep him informed. He informed us that Federal troops had already been sent to Fort McClellan, just on the edge of Anniston, to be there in case they were needed in Birmingham where the situation was very critical following the explosion of the bomb that killed the four children at the Sixteenth Street Baptist Church.

Following our visit to Nimrod's home and the telephone conversation with President Kennedy, Claude, Miller, Charlie and I discussed our next step. What should we do? We discussed what would happen in Anniston if the plans to desegregate the library were thwarted. If the KKK and a hoodlum mob could keep the city from integrating the library now, they could well use similar tactics to block any other changes relating to race. A consensus quickly emerged. It was absolutely essential that we go on with plans to desegregate the library. We had to make crystal clear to the citizens of Anniston, and especially to the hoodlums, that the city was not going to be run by mobs! So we planned that the next day, Monday afternoon, we would escort two black ministers into the library.

This time we took no chance. Claude and Miller would talk to Police Commissioner Jack Suggs about police protection. Even though every attempt had been made to keep the original plans secret, somehow the Klan and other hoodlums had learned about the plans. Certainly the police also knew. I feel strongly that the police knew full well not only of the plans for the Library desegregation but also of the Klan's plan for a violent response. It was telling that the police did not arrive on the scene until the violence was over. As we have learned over the years, this was an all-too common situation in the 1950s and 1960s where Southern police departments and the KKK were concerned. In both Birmingham and Montgomery in 1961, for example, it has since been proven that police officials collaborated with KKK elements to allow time for arriving Freedom Riders to be brutally beaten by mobs at the bus stations in these respective cities before police showed up to restore order. Ample evidence has been revealed of Southern police officers who were also KKK members and there is no doubt in my mind that we had some of this in Anniston.

As Claude, Miller, Charlie and I made plans we wanted to be absolutely sure there was police protection. Jack Suggs pledged his support to maintain order and to see that there would be no mob violence Monday afternoon. The plan was that the Mayor would not walk into the Library with us, but that Miller, Charlie, and I would go with the two black ministers. Both Nimrod and Bob wanted to be the ones to go into the Library, however Nimrod, who had been the most badly beaten, was not physically able. George Smitherman, pastor of Mt. Calvary Baptist Church, who had also been very active in working for civil rights, was to go with Bob. The plan was that several policemen would be stationed in the Library and that police patrol cars would circle the block in which the Library was located. If the situation seemed to be under control by the police, then about 3 p.m., Miller would call me at my church office and I would join him, Charlie, Bob, and George in the parking lot adjacent to the Library and together we would walk down the sidewalk in front of the Library and turn down the walk that led into the Library, just as Nimrod and Bob had done the previous day.

Miller called and before I could get out of the church, he called again saying, "Come right now. Things are under control, but people are around and we do not know when it might change." I went as quickly as I could get there. When I got to the parking lot, I was surprised to find that Mrs. Lucian Lentz, a strong, active library board member, was there and intended to walk with us. It was important for her, a Jewish woman, to make her witness against prejudice and discrimination. I remember feeling proud of her and moved by her courage.

As we walked to the Library I was conscious of a few ruffians being around, but they simply stood and looked. As we went in the front door, there was a man seated just inside who glared at us with anger and hatred, but he remained seated. I was very careful not to walk too close to him.

The plan was for Bob and George to each check out a book and we would all leave the Library together. Bob asked for a copy of *How Far the Promised Land?* When it was not available he checked out the book entitled, *If I Had Only One Sermon to Preach*. George checked out a copy of *Blood, Sweat and Tears*. Obviously both had carefully considered the symbol of the book they chose.

Thus the first step of many toward dismantling the system of segregation had been taken in Anniston. We had demonstrated that the City was not going to be run by hoodlum mobs! In addition, rewards totaling nineteen hundred dollars were offered for information leading to the

arrest and conviction of white mobsters involved in the Sunday afternoon terrorism.

I did not know until I read Monday's *Anniston Star* that the attack at
the Library on Sunday apparently had spawned at least two other racial
violence incidents that night. Frank Brown, a white man who lived on
Christine Avenue, was attacked and beaten by five teenage blacks as he
walked along West Fifteenth Street. He was treated at the hospital for a
scalp wound inflicted by a bottle and was released. Vera Young, the
operator of a black cafe in Central City, just west of Anniston, told police
that three shotgun blasts were fired into the cafe by unknown persons at
about 10:30 p.m.

Monday's *Star* also contained a statement I had issued Sunday
afternoon, as chairman of the Human Relations Council, strongly
condemning the afternoon violence:

> We deeply regret the injury that has come to two of our local citizens
> who have been trying to work with the people of the Negro race and
> those of the white race to bring about a wise and workable solution to
> our problems. The ugly deed this afternoon must not happen again in
> the City of Anniston. It is the same kind of cowardly action that has
> taken place in other communities and now in ours. Arrests and convic-
> tions must be made. The citizens of Anniston must do everything in
> their power to see that this is done. No citizen of Anniston is safe as long
> as this type of thing can be done successfully. I am confident that plans
> originally made by the Library Board at the direction of a majority of the
> City Commission will be carried through. I am also confident that there
> are enough responsible citizens in our city who will both speak and act
> to displace such an outrage with good, hard common sense and toler-
> ance. May the Lord have mercy upon us if such is not the case.[37]

It was encouraging to have the Session of the First Presbyterian
Church on October 27 pass a motion saying "that all the members of the
Human Relations Council be commended for the work that they have
done."[38] Commendation also came from President Kennedy, who wrote

Mayor Dear on October 2: "I have your letter of September 28 together with the newspaper clippings and I am delighted to note the responsible manner in which the city administration has been handling some difficult and delicate problems."[39]

The police department moved rapidly to make arrests in the September 15 attack on Nimrod and Bob at the Library. They also made an arrest in the attack on the white man, Frank Brown, who had been assaulted by the teenagers that night. All these arrests were made on Thursday following the Sunday incidents.

Four white men were arrested and booked on two charges each of assault with intent to murder. Warrants were signed by Nimrod and Bob against Billy Franklin Young, 26; Mike Fox, 44; Willie Waugh, 45; and a fourth person whose name is not available. (Fox had been arrested previously in connection with an attack on the singer Nat King Cole, in Birmingham in 1956, as had Anniston KKK leader Kenneth Adams.) A black youth, Terrell Reed, 17, was arrested and charged with assault with intent to murder for the attack on Frank Brown. (To my knowledge, no arrests were ever made in connection with the shotgun blasts at the Central City cafe.)

After a hearing at Anniston's Recorder's Court on the following Saturday, the four white suspects were bound over to the grand jury under ten thousand dollars bond each. Terrell Reed and three other black youths that by then had also been arrested for the attack on Frank Brown were bound over to the grand jury under five thousand dollars bond each.

Although Police Commissioner Jack Suggs had voted against the formation of the biracial Human Relations Council and had made it clear that he was not in favor of integration, his swift action in making these arrests demonstrated that violence, regardless of its motivation or source, would not be tolerated in Anniston. This official reaction helped put a cap on what could have been a serious escalation of the racial events of violence that occurred on Sunday, September 15.

Meanwhile, though the arrests were significant in themselves, the community waited to see what the courts would do. While four white men were bound over to the grand jury, only Billy Franklin Young was indicted. Of the four black youths bound over to the grand jury, only Isaiah Harris, Jr., was indicted. And the indictments against Young and Harris were later dismissed, as related in an article in the *Anniston Star* on November 13, 1963:

> Circuit Solicitor Clarence Williams Tuesday dropped charges against two young men indicted by a grand jury for racial violence here Sept. 15. The solicitor said dismissal of the cases was recommended by the victims of beatings on that Sunday, when two of the victims attempted to integrate Carnegie Library.
>
> Charges were dismissed against Billy Franklin Young, 26, of 2515 Wilmer Ave., and Negro Isiah Harris, Jr., 17, of R-3 Cooper Homes, both charged with assault with intent to murder.
>
> An observer, who declined to be identified, pointed out that the solicitor was not bound by the recommendation of the victims, and could have prosecuted the defendants had he desired. [Williams] pointed out the "racial clashes involved crimes against society in general and were not personal feuds between the defendants and the victims." Solicitor Williams, discussing the cases, said he thinks all those involved "feel like getting this thing settled down."
>
> Four white men, including Young, were bound over to the last session of the grand jury on charges of attacking the Revs. William B. McClain and N. Quintus Reynolds, both Negroes, as they approached Carnegie Library.
>
> Four Negro teen-agers including Harris, were bound over on charges they beat Frank Brown, a white man, as he walked along West 15th Street in a Negro section later that day.
>
> The grand jury failed to bring indictments against three of the whites and three of the Negroes. In a statement to Solicitor Williams recommending that prosecution of Young be dropped, the two Negro ministers indicated disappointment at the failure of the grand jury to indict all accused of attacking them. The statement, in part reads as follows: "Whereas it was the decision of the grand jury to fail to indict all of the

four persons bound over to them from the city court on the charges of
. . . assault with intent to murder . . . And . . . there is no doubt in our
minds of the involvement of each of the four persons . . . And . . .
conviction does not seem imminent in the case of the fourth person . . .
We therefore recommend that the charges be dropped on the . . . fourth
person, Billy Franklin Young." It [the statement] is dated Nov. 12 and
signed by Revs. McClain and Reynolds.

The solicitor said Brown had recommended dropping the charges
against Harris.[40]

The black community was keenly disappointed that the grand jury
did not indict all four white men arrested in connection with the library
attack. Given the past pattern of white people not being convicted for
crimes against blacks, the inaction was no surprise to the black community. However, considering that dozens of hoodlums had participated in
the attack on Reynolds and McClain, the subsequent prosecution of only
one assailant was seen as a further symbol of injustice to the black
community. The fact that charges were also dismissed against one of the
black youths arrested for attacking the white man on the same day
probably eased but could not heal the resentment within the black
community over the dismissal of charges against the other white men
arrested in the library attack.

The stage was set for more violence. The strong enforcement of law
and order by Commissioner Suggs and the constant work by the Human
Relations Council played a part in keeping the violence to a minimum.
While the library attack helped the community to see the evil of hatred
and racism, and perhaps marked a turning point, there were still major
problems to be solved, hopefully without more violence.

10

Slow Progress, But Progress

THE EVENTS OF 1963 set the course the city would take in dealing with its racial problems. The Civil Rights Movement was in full bloom, and many other Southern cities and towns were marked by continuing conflict and violence. But Anniston had made clear that it intended to solve its problems by communication between the races, negotiated changes, and enforcement of law and order. We would see in 1964 and 1965 whether our approach would work. We knew it surely would be tested.

By 1964 white and colored signs had been removed from rest rooms and drinking fountains. Some lunch counters had been desegregated. The library had been opened to blacks, and in the process it had been shown that mobs and hoodlums would not prevail, but that the city would be governed by its elected officials. Law and order would be enforced even by a police commissioner who was not in favor of integration.

Gradual desegregation followed of the theaters, the municipal golf course, and some restaurants. All of this occurred without loss of life or even serious injury, however there were some bombings. On February 27, a dynamite blast knocked radio station WDNG off the air for about an hour. More damage was done to the building housing the station than to the transmitting equipment. The owner of the station, Tom Potts, had been broadcasting editorials calling for law and order, and advocating a moderate approach to racial integration. Anniston Hardware Company, owned by Miller Sproull, who had taken a leadership role in appointing the Human Relations Council, was also bombed. Fortunately it was a poorly set dynamite charge and only the entranceway of the building was damaged. A tear-gas bomb exploded in Rose's variety store, spreading burning, acrid fumes which drove customers and store personnel from the building. Rose's was one of three stores that had integrated their lunch counters several weeks previously.

These acts of violence notwithstanding, progress continued to be made and attitudes and actions were steadily changing. The Chamber of Commerce, concerned for the economic aspects of Anniston, met with members of the black community to discuss employment concerns. Edward Wood reported that at one such meeting forty-eight jobs were promised. When the jobs were not forthcoming, Mayor Dear met with and chastised the Chamber of Commerce members for promising and not delivering. Wood said the black community recognized the Mayor as "standing up for them."

Wood also described some of the changes taking place in the pipe shops and foundries. The foundries had showers where the employees cleaned up at the end of their shifts before they went home. The shower area had a partition dividing it into "white" and "colored" shower areas. One day management simply knocked out the partition. Nothing else changed, and apparently black workers were still reluctant to use the side that had been for white workers. Wood recalled the day he and another black man stepped into the white side, where a white man was already beneath the shower. Wood, somewhat nervous himself, said to the white man, "Is the water hot?" He relates with amusement that the equally nervous white man stepped out from under the water, and then stuck his hand back into the shower and said, "Yeah, it's hot."[41]

The formerly white Anniston Ministerial Association had sponsored a citywide Thanksgiving service across denominational lines for many years. The service, of course, had been attended only by whites. Now that the Ministerial Association was integrated its citywide service would include both black and white worshippers. I was president of the

Ministerial Association at this time and the Session of First Presbyterian
Church agreed to have the service in its sanctuary. Everything went well
and many blacks attended. Some of the older members of our ushering
group tended to seat the black visitors all in a group, but there was
nevertheless a general distribution in the seating pattern. It was a very
small step forward.

The Ministerial Association also had been sponsoring noontime Holy
Week community services. It was decided that these integrated services
would be held in the City Hall rather than in one of the churches. Again,
things went very well in these services with both black and white
ministers leading them. There were always police guards in and around
the City Hall. It did feel a bit strange for blacks and whites to be doing
the service together, but it also felt strange to have to have police guards
for protection of a worship service. It also felt strange to be having the
services in a secular city hall, rather than in one of our churches.

Opinions in the community were quite divided about the movement
to integration. The black community thought we were going too slow,
and the white community thought we were going too fast. Opinions
were not monolithic *within* the two communities, either, and our
churches were no exception. This is illustrated by conversations I had
with two members of First Presbyterian. The clerk of our Session,
attorney Richard Emerson, felt that it was right to integrate our churches
since openness to all people was consistent with the Gospel, but that we
"had no business" trying to integrate secular society. About that same
time, congregant Marshall Hunter, who was president of the First
National Bank, told me he thought it was right to bring integration to
secular society, but the church was private and it should not be integrated. It was around this same time when Mayor Claude Dear told me
that a joke making its rounds in the city went like this: "Do you know
how to be a good Presbyterian? Take a Nigger to lunch."[42]

The feelings involved could become extremely sensitive.

E. L. Turner, Jr., was a strong and respected elder of First Presbyterian
Church. He was chairman of the committee to build our new church.
We were together often as we worked through details of our building

program. I was extremely fond of and had tremendous respect for Mr. Turner. He had never said anything to me about my involvement on the Human Relations Council until one day in the church's parking lot after one of our meetings he "had a talk" with me. He cited the dangers of integration saying that it would lead to intermarriage. He declared that South America had mingled the races and the result was that South Americans were generally inferior to the Caucasians of North America. He also said that a study of history would show that where the Negro race had mingled with another race, the result was a diminution of the race with which it had mingled.

I replied that I did not know the outcome or ultimate results of the civil rights revolution that was going on in the South and in Anniston, and the only thing I knew to do was to try to do what I thought was the Christian thing in this situation and with any other issue in which I was involved. With some apparent irritation, Mr. Turner said, "Phil, you are as ignorant of ethnology as I am of the Bible." Of course, this was an incorrect statement on his part, as I was almost totally ignorant of ethnology, while he was quite knowledgeable of the Bible.

I regretted that we viewed the issue of race so differently, because though he was old enough to be my father I felt a strong bond of friendship with him. He and his close friend, C. M. Jesperson, had a fishing lake about six miles outside Anniston toward Jacksonville. Mr. Turner would occasionally invite me to go fishing. I was not much of a fisherman and neither was he. He was a Princeton University graduate and he had continued to grow intellectually through reading and travel. I always stood in amazement of his breath and depth of knowledge. I think he took me fishing so he could expose "his minister" to some of the many things he felt I needed to know. He was the essence of a Southern gentleman and began many conversations by saying, "Phil, do you know . . ." such and such a quotation? I seldom ever knew the quotation but I always answered, "No, Mr. Turner, I do not know that one," as if I knew most, but not that particular one. One day as he was experiencing some health problems, and no longer was able to go to Europe as he had done nearly every summer for many years, he said to me as we were sitting in the fishing boat, some minnow having long since nibbled away our bait, "Phil, do you know Robert Browning's poem, 'Grow old along with me, the best is yet to be'?" I replied, "Yes, Mr. Turner, I do know that poem." He said with emphasis, "It's the biggest lie that was ever told!"

I learned much from Mr. Turner. One day as we were fishing I said, "Mr. Turner, you have lived a long time and I think you are very wise. What do you think is the most important thing in life?" He was quiet for several long minutes, and then he said, "I don't know." The next day he came to my office and said to me, "I have been thinking a lot about the question you asked me yesterday. I think the answer is FAMILY."

There was always an ache in my heart because we perceived the race issue so differently.

Of course the racial attitudes of Mr. Turner were mild compared to the views of many who were determined to thwart even small steps toward equal rights. It was abundantly clear that additional violence was a possibility as desegregation of community institutions proceeded. It was perhaps this sense of uncertainty about potential violence that led Mayor Claude Dear to say to me in early 1964, "I wish it was possible for you and Kenneth Adams to talk to each other."

Local KKK leader Kenneth Adams's name was synonymous with much of the racial violence in the Anniston area and even in Birmingham. I remember the look of surprise that came over Claude's face when I replied that I would be willing to meet with Adams. Claude said he would try to arrange a meeting, and he did. On the appointed day, Kenneth Adams came out to my office, then in the Lanford house that was on the property we had bought to build the new church. Adams arrived about 5:30 P.M., when the secretary and others had gone, and I was there by myself. Kenneth Adams was born in 1920 and was thus one year older than me. He was dressed in a khaki shirt and khaki pants. He was partially bald with a lock of brown hair on his middle forehead. I was surprised to find him a bit softspoken and polite. By his appearance and demeanor, I would never have guessed him to be the violent racist that he was. We talked together for about an hour, and it was a surprisingly low-key meeting. He showed no anger, nor did either of us ever raise our

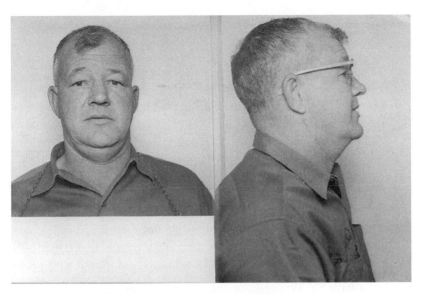

Police photos of Kenneth Adams, about 1963.

voices. He talked about his attitudes about blacks, obviously considering them very inferior and almost sub-human. He asked me if I thought they had souls. I replied, "Yes." Then he asked if I had ever observed "niggers" when they were scared? I said that I had not. He then described, with what seemed to be some amusement and even relish, his observations of how blacks acted when they were afraid. I explained my views, which were so different from his, and indicated that what we—the Council and other city leaders—were trying to do was to give black people the same opportunities that whites had. We observed that obviously he was doing what he thought should be done for the white race and the community, and I was doing what I thought should be done. When he left, we shook hands in a remarkably cordial manner.

After that meeting, the late-night calls to me reduced considerably. A few weeks afterward, Adams was in jail for something and he called me from the jail to tell me his situation and to ask if I could do anything to get him out. I told him I would talk to the authorities and do what I could, which I did. I believe my meeting with Kenneth Adams "put a human face" on the situation and probably reduced the chances that I would be the object of violence.

In retrospect, it might have been naïve of me to meet alone with Kenneth Adams, considering the violence he had created and participated in, and considering that the Ku Klux Klan had discussed how they might kill me and others involved in Anniston's desegregation efforts. As I think back on this encounter it reminds me of the episode in my father's life, when he faced the person who had said he was going to kill him. I did not really take many precautions during this period, except for checking my car when I first used it in the mornings. I went about my normal life and it would have been relatively easy to do me harm.

Our family car was a white Chevrolet station wagon, which made life possible when we traveled as a family. We would put one child in the front seat with me, one child in the back seat with Betty, and the third child in the seat in the very back. This reduced bickering to a level that Betty and I could tolerate. As a minister, I had to come and go a lot so we also had a second car, a 1957 second-hand blue Hillman-Minx convertible with white sidewall tires. This was a rather strange, small British car and was the only one like it in Anniston. In those days, round stiff straw hats were back in style (or at least I thought they were) and I remember riding down Noble Street with the top down and wearing my straw boater hat! I must have been quite a sight. My point, though, is that I was not inconspicuous or hard to find in Anniston. I was easily identifiable if any of the thugs or hoodlums had decided to carry out their threats.

I love to hunt quail and hunting in that part of Alabama was fairly good. Often in the afternoons I went hunting by myself. I would get into the blue Hillman-Minx, put my bird dogs Esau and Jacob in the trunk, and off I would go to the farm of a friend or someone who would permit me to hunt on their land. It would have been very easy for someone to follow and kill me without witnesses, and the same is probably true for most of the other members of the Human Relations Council. Perhaps I should have been more careful, but in the good providence of God, I and a number of others who were threatened, were not harmed.

The more success we had locally in changing segregation patterns, the more outsiders came in to stir up opposition. Among those were J. B. Stoner and the Rev. Connie Lynch. One day when I was at the City Hall, I saw a member of First Presbyterian Church with two men that I did not know. As I walked by I spoke to the church member. He said to me, "Phil, meet these people from Atlanta. They are Mr. Stoner and Mr. Lynch." Their names did not mean much to me until I reached out my hand to shake hands with them, just as is ordinarily done when men are introduced. It was only when they refused to shake hands, that their names clicked in my mind: J. B. Stoner and Connie Lynch! The member who introduced us was a friend of mine, but clearly a racist, as I had known for some time. However, I didn't think he was a "Stoner or Lynch" type racist. No conversation followed the introduction.

Stoner was an Atlanta lawyer and active in something called the National States Rights Party, an anti-black, anti-Jewish organization with strong links to the KKK and neo-Nazi groups. Stoner was no stranger to Anniston, as is illustrated by an *Anniston Star* article that appeared some weeks after the 1961 Freedom Riders bus burning just outside of town. The article (see appendix) described a white supremacist rally during which effigies of several civil rights leaders and federal officials were hanged. The rally protested the federal grand jury indictment of Kenneth Adams and eight others for their roles in attacking and burning the Greyhound bus on which the Freedom Riders had been passengers.

The almost unbelievable attitude of Connie Lynch is revealed in statements he made after the four girls were killed in the Birmingham church bombing. He was quoted in the press as saying the Klansmen responsible deserved "medals" and that the four girls "weren't children. Children are little people, little human beings, and that means white people . . . They're just little niggers . . . and if there's four less niggers tonight, then I say, 'Good for whoever planted the bomb.'"[43]

On May 1, 1964, Dr. Martin Luther King, Jr., soon to receive the Nobel Peace Prize, spoke at the Seventeenth Street Baptist Church, commending the black leadership of Anniston, specifically recognizing Nimrod Reynolds and Bob McClain for their efforts. By this time, the

Calhoun County Improvement Association, a black organization created to work toward racial justice and better opportunities for their race, and affiliated with King's Southern Christian Leadership Conference, had been in existence for one year.

Progress was being made in Anniston, but it could not come fast enough. On September 13, 1964, the Calhoun County Improvement Association took out a full-page ad in the *Anniston Star* to publish a remarkable document entitled "Anniston Manifesto" (see Appendix). Citing the Declaration of Independence, the Constitution, the Bible, and quotations from King and John Oxenham, the manifesto was an impassioned plea for fairness now rather than later. The manifesto also pointedly referred to Anniston's designation as a "Model City" of America and declared that blacks wanted to and deserved to be full citizens of their home town.

A local man named Charlie Keyes, who had become the self-appointed spokesman for segregationists and who often paraded in front of the schools with pro-segregation signs as the schools were being integrated, quickly responded on September 19 with an issue of his newsletter, "The Keyes Report," which was widely distributed in Anniston. In an issue entitled "Reply to Anniston Manifesto," he warned that integration was already happening too quickly and that the destruction of the country and the mongrelization of the races would be the inevitable result. (See Appendix).

Interestingly, Keyes paid a probably unintentional compliment to the Human Relations Council when he declared, "Few people realize how much integration has taken place since the formation of the bi-racial committee because it hasn't been publicized. But, so far, the water fountains and rest rooms of many businesses have been integrated, next the library, the variety store lunch counters, the municipal golf course, the theatres and some of the restaurants, and some colored people have attended many of the heretofore white churches."

Well, we had certainly been trying to accomplish all that. Despite the understandable feeling of the black community that progress was too slow and the equally understandable if lamentable reaction of extremists like Charlie Keyes, who unfortunately spoke for too many people, the Human Relations Council continued its deliberate work of communication and negotiation.

However, the extremists and the influence of their hatefilled rhetoric were not yet finished.

On March 20, 1965, Dr. Gordon Rodgers and Nimrod Reynolds filed a discrimination lawsuit against Anniston Memorial Hospital seeking to end the operation of racially segregated wards. There followed in reaction to this and other developments a new round of white supremacist rallies, always with vitriolic speeches by some of those already mentioned. On July 15, such a rally was held at the Calhoun County Courthouse in Anniston. About a hundred Klan members and sympathizers gathered that night to hear a parade of speakers that included J. B. Stoner, Charlie Keyes, Kenneth Adams, and Dr. Ed Fields, a virulently anti-semitic chiropractor from the Atlanta area who was a Stoner associate in the National States Rights Party. The night's most rabid comments may have been uttered by the Rev. Connie Lynch, who was quoted as saying, "If it takes killing to get the Negroes out of the white man's streets and to protect our constitutional rights, then I say yes, kill them."[44]

Apparently incited by what they had heard at the rally, a group of several white men left the event and randomly shot into a car carrying three black workers home from their shift at an Anniston pipe foundry. One of the bullets lodged in the spine of the thirty-eight-year-old driver, Willie Brewster. The other passengers were uninjured and managed to get the car under control—and observed that their attackers were several white men—but Brewster died two days later. His wife, pregnant with the couple's third child, went into shock and had a miscarriage. [See Appendix, "The Willie Brewster Murder"]

The senselessness of this shooting incident shocked the Anniston community and galvanized people into action. Within twelve hours, twenty thousand dollars in reward money had been raised and the *Anniston Star* editorialized that the reward offer "says to Willie Brewster and to the world that he is not alone at this moment, that the persons who brought him to the point of death . . . are not just his enemies. They are enemies of us all, and we stand together in opposition to them."

It is interesting how the reward money was raised by the community. The next day after the shooting of Brewster, Dr. T. C. Donald, a prominent Anniston physician, called Brandt Ayers at the *Anniston Star* and said, "We've got to do something." Brandt and his wife Josephine and a few others met at Dr. Donald's house at six o'clock that evening, and it was decided to offer a reward of twenty thousand dollars, which was quite a sum at that time. They also agreed to make telephone calls to Anniston citizens asking them three things: Will you contribute money toward the reward? Will you be willing for your name to be included in a full page ad in the *Star* deploring the killing of Brewster? Will you call three other people and ask for their participation? By midnight that night the twenty thousand dollars had been pledged and a list of three hundred names, most of them well-known citizens, had been secured. The following Sunday the ad appeared in which three hundred names declared: WE ARE DETERMINED THAT THOSE WHO ADVOCATE AND COMMIT SECRET ACTS OF VIOLENCE WILL NOT CONTROL THIS COMMUNITY.

The *Star* followed up for several days with a front-page graphic instructing potential reward claimants how to anonymously place a classified ad for a lost dog with a crippled hind leg, signed with a series of numbers and letters and urging anyone with information to communicate with the authorities or the *Star*. Eventually the classified ad appeared indicating that the informant had communicated with the authorities.

Lured by the reward money, a white man named Jimmy Knight came forward to testify that he had been at the white supremacist rally with Hubert Damon Strange. Knight reported that as Strange, Johnny Ira Defries, Lewis Blevins, and Bill Rozier rode with him in his car on the night Willie Brewster was shot, Strange said, "We got us a nigger tonight." Someone in the car said, "Damon put a pumpkin ball in a nigger's head." Damon commented, "Yeah, I had to lean halfway out of the window to get a shot." Knight said he asked Damon, "How many did you get?" Damon replied, "I know I got the driver cause the car veered to the left, I believe it went into a ditch."[45]

Strange, 23, was an employee of Kenneth Adams. Indicted with Strange in August 1965 were Defries and Blevins. An all-white jury subsequently convicted Strange (after thirteen hours deliberation and twenty ballots) of second-degree murder and sentenced him to ten years in prison. Co-defendant Defries was acquitted in a second trial. Information about Blevins is sketchy, but it appears that his case was dismissed in exchange for his cooperation and testimony.

There is a sequel to the story about Johnny Defries. He was well known by the police as one who was fascinated with Volkswagens and especially Volkswagen beetles. He stole many of them. It was said he could steal one and remove the motor in a matter of minutes. Sometime after being acquitted in the Brewster murder trial, Defries was arrested for murder in connection with a barroom brawl and was sent to prison. He later escaped and the Anniston police department was notified. Information was received that Defries was with his girl friend in a mobile home west of Anniston off Highway 202. Gary Carroll and Steve Robinson of the Anniston police department, along with several FBI agents and possibly with an agent from the State Bureau of Investigation, went to the mobile home. Carroll and Robinson went to the front door while the others went to the back door. When they knocked on the door two girls opened the door. The officers identified themselves as police officers, and asked if Johnny Defries was there. The girls said, "No." A search of the mobile home was made and Defries was not found. The girls indicated he had been there and they expected him to return.

The FBI agents hid in the woods around the mobile home while Carroll and Robinson sat in the living room talking to the two girls as they waited for Defries. There was no air conditioning in the mobile home and inside it was very hot and stuffy. Carroll became very relaxed and drowsy sitting with his shotgun across his knees. After a while Robinson went into the kitchen to get a drink of water. He noticed on the counter an open beer can that had condensation on it, indicating it had not been out of the refrigerator very long. Robinson thought to himself that Defries probably would not just go off and leave half a can of cold beer. As he then looked around in the kitchen he thought he saw something move in the corner where there were some garbage sacks. Then he spotted Defries's shoe. He pulled his pistol and yelled for Defries to get up. The sudden yell so surprised Carroll in the living room that he almost dropped his shotgun. Defries was handcuffed and returned to prison.[46]

Jimmy Glen Knight, who informed on Willie Brewster's murderers, had contacted Joe Landers of the FBI. Landers contacted Harry Sims, the state investigator who handled the Brewster case. Sims got the twenty thousand dollars reward money from the First National Bank and gave a check for that amount to Knight, who immediately left Anniston and was said to have gone to Florida.[47]

Hubert Damon Strange never went to prison because he was killed in a bar fight while out on bond pending appeal of his conviction. Brandt Ayers tells some interesting details about how Strange was killed. "At a dive out on Highway 202, Strange drew a pistol on the man he suspected of informing on him, but the shot missed. The man bolted out the back door and Strange followed. Strange steadied his aim on the door frame and fired, but there had been only one bullet in the chamber. Later, while his case was on appeal, Strange drew his pistol on another man at another dive, but the other man was quicker. Strange was fatally wounded. He lived with violence and died violently."[48]

At his trial, Strange had been represented by white supremacist attorney J. B. Stoner, who had been one of the speakers at the rally which incited Brewster's murderers. During the trial Josephine Ayers interviewed Stoner and quoted him as saying that the only thing he had against Hitler was that Hitler didn't kill all the six million Jews he was said to have exterminated.[49]

It is important to note that, for all the violence that white people inflicted on black people during the civil rights era, this was the very first time that a white person was convicted of killing a black person in Alabama. The verdict by a Calhoun County jury may have been influenced by the changing attitudes that resulted from the work of the Human Relations Council. Of course, the horror and senselessness of arbitrarily killing an innocent man just because he was black caused revulsion in the black and most of the white community. But bad things had happened in the past and the white perpetrators were not convicted. The conviction of Strange thus marked some progress.

The various indictments and trials during this period caused City Attorney Richard Emerson, an elder in the First Presbyterian Church, to express concern about the rolls from which local jurors were selected. He observed to Brandt Ayers that not a single one of the three hundred signers of the reward ad were on the jury rolls. An investigation followed and it was found that the three-member jury commission was composed of one man known to be a racist, a one-legged blind man who ran a little store in the courthouse lobby, and a conscientious citizen from Piedmont, a nearby Calhoun County town. Among the names in the jury pool were convicted felons and known racists! There were few blacks. The investigation and its findings led to a reform of the jury system in Calhoun County.[50]

There were these horrible incidents in Anniston, but there was not widespread violence, and communication continued through the Human Relations Council. In time, there would be major problems at Walter Welborn High School and at the Anniston Memorial Hospital. But a pattern had been set for Anniston not to tear itself apart, but to work through its problems with communication and negotiation.

The Human Relations Council had been appointed originally for only one year, so the city commission could easily dismantle it if the experiment had not worked out. The original Council, appointed on May 16, 1963, was reappointed in 1964 and was coming up for reappointment again in May 1965. Though the city commission indicated its desire for me to continue on the Council, I wrote Mayor Dear in April [see Appendix], expressing my appreciation for having been allowed to serve but indicating my wish to resign:

Many good results have attended our work—results which at the beginning we hoped for, but without any assurance that they would come. Without attempting to detail any of these good results, I simply point to the fact that during the last two years cities and communities all about us have had untold racial problems dealt with at the conference table. It is my hope that a pattern has been set in dealing with our problems which will increasingly result in community good will, fairness, and wholeness. Since I have now served for two years, and since it is our opinion that some new members should be appointed each year, thereby broadening the base of support for the council and also distributing the responsibility for its work; therefore, I shall not accept further appointment to the Human Relations Council upon the expiration of this year's term.[51]

As I completed these two years, I gave thanks that none of the original members of the Human Relations Council had suffered violence beyond that which happened to Nimrod and Bob at the library "incident." We all knew from the beginning that such was possible and maybe probable. I also gave thanks that though there had been sporadic violence in our community during these years, we had not suffered the widespread violence that had occurred in many other towns. At one point, the neighboring town of Gadsden was having racial troubles and blacks there had distributed a flyer urging people not to shop in Gadsden but to shop instead in Anniston where a more open and fair city respected blacks as human beings.

Anniston during these two years had gone through some changes, and these changes were in the right direction. For all of that, I was grateful to God.

II

In Retrospect

LOOKING BACK OVER THE DECADE from the mid-1950s to the mid-1960s from the perspective of almost four decades later reveals some interesting things. There were factors that enabled the Human Relations Council's work to be successful and others that made the work more difficult.

One of the positive aspects was that all of the members of the original Council were local people who had been in Anniston a long time. Bob McClain and I were perhaps the newcomers and I had been there for seven years. There was a widespread rejection of people who came in from the outside, whether it was black or white. There was a feeling that problems should be worked out locally. The Human Relations Council was composed of local people who had been a part of the community for a number of years. It was local people working at local problems.

Those appointed were respected in their communities. The black community was well represented. Nimrod Reynolds, pastor of the Seventeenth Street Baptist Church, had been the minister there for some time and was a leader in his community. Bob McClain was pastor of the Haven Chapel Methodist Church and was a very intelligent and articulate leader in his community. Grant Oden was a leader in a black labor union. Raleigh Byrd was a long-time citizen of Anniston, and owned a dry-cleaning business, and represented the more established and conservative element in the black community.

The white members represented a wide spectrum of interests and influence. Leonard Roberts was from an old, respected family in Anniston. As executive in one of the primary industries in Anniston, he represented the economic aspect of the community. Marcus Howze, president of the Commercial National Bank, represented the considerable financial interests of the community. Wilfred Galbraith was not only part of an influential and respected family in the community but was the editor of the *Anniston Star* and had much to do with information that circulated in the community. Edwin Cosper was a close friend of Mayor Dear and, in some sense, was a representative of the westside white community. As for myself, I had been the minister of First Presbyterian Church for seven years and was president of the white Ministerial Association. All in all, it was good, strong, and broad representation of the community.

At one point, Leonard Roberts said to me, "Phil, I know you want us to solve our racial problems on religious grounds, and because you think it is right. But if they are solved it is going to be because of economics." To an extent I had to agree with him, and I was glad he was there representing the economic aspect of the community. We certainly would not have made the progress we did without the support of the economic community and the Chamber of Commerce. I felt that in Anniston the business and religious communities worked together to effect needed changes.

The support of the black ministers in the community was almost unanimous, while the support of the white ministers was mixed. The pattern of support revealed an interesting and somewhat disturbing phenomenon. With few exceptions, the black ministers were serving Baptist churches and therefore served at the will of their congregations. Since blacks were almost universally in favor of the removal of the patterns of segregation, the Baptist ministers and those serving churches with congregational type of government also served at the will of their congregation. However, most Southern whites in 1963 were opposed to integration, so any white minister in churches with congregational government who took an outspoken stand for integration was in danger of losing his job. Pastors of Presbyterian, Episcopal, Catholic, and

Methodist churches who had either a bishop or presbytery to be accountable to were protected in a sense by their form of government. Therefore, the general pattern was that black Baptist pastors spoke out and led in desegregation. But in the white community the Baptist ministers and others with a congregational form of government were not generally supportive of desegregation, while the most outspoken and supportive were in churches with bishops and presbyteries. Unless the bishops were segregationists, and most were not, there was not much danger of the minister losing his job.

It is interesting that when I met a couple of years ago with a small group of black ministers and lay friends to discuss the things that happened in the decade from the mid-1950s to the mid-1960s, they brought out the fact that not many white Baptist ministers were involved in the civil rights movement. But in characteristic black practicality and tolerance they said: "But we understood. They might have lost their jobs." Having made this analysis, integrity requires me to ask, "Would I have taken the lead I did if I had been serving a church with congregational form of government?" I can only answer, "I hope so."

We like to think that ministers are so committed to the Gospel and the Bible's call for justice that they would be unaffected by the lack of security. There were, of course, many exceptions where ministers spoke out in spite of being at risk of losing their jobs. And we must acknowledge that some white ministers were segregationists themselves. On the other hand, many black lay people were dependent upon whites for their jobs, and therefore were not outspoken for fear of losing their jobs. But their true attitude came out in their strong support of civil rights in their churches and in the support of their pastors. And many courageous black men and women who supported the movement did speak out despite the risk of losing their jobs.

The old saying "it's hard to get the first olive out of the bottle" was sometimes applied to the difficulty of getting someone to be willing to take the lead in changing the segregation patterns. Once someone is willing to do this, it makes it easier for others to follow. The nine original members of the Human Relations Council were like those first olives.

Mayor Dear and Commissioner Miller Sproull also come in that category.

Miller Sproull was the key person in bringing about the appointment of the Human Relations Council. Mayor Dear spoke of Miller's influence on him saying, "I think Miller Sproull is the smartest person I have ever known." While Mayor Dear was for having a Human Relations Council, the fact that Miller was a strong and consistent advocate of a Council gave the Mayor the support he needed to appoint the Council. The simple fact is that I do not believe there would have been a Bi-racial Human Relations Council if it had not been for Miller Sproull.

The appointment of the bi-racial Human Relations Council was a crucial key in opening and keeping open official communication between the races in Anniston. The mayor and city commissioners were wise and courageous enough to appoint the Council, whereas other communities refused to do so. Typical of the attitude in other cities and towns was that of Mayor Allen Thompson of Jackson, Mississippi. He announced to "a conference he had called with seventy-five white business leaders . . . No biracial committee will be appointed in Jackson . . . The only thing that can come from such an arrangement is compliance with the demands of racial agitators from the outside."[52]

The role played by Anniston Police Commissioner Jack Suggs was interesting and critical. Jack made it clear he was not in favor of integration nor in favor of appointing the Human Relations Council. He voted against it. However, he also made it clear that he intended for his police department to enforce the law, and that included what the City Commission passed, regardless of whether the offenders were white or black. He did not have the "Bull Connor" mentality (Bull Connor was the police chief in Birmingham who used fire hoses and police dogs on demonstrators). Suggs's resolute determination to enforce the law for all people gave a stability that would not have otherwise been possible.

It was fortunate that among the first appointees to the Human Relations Council was Wilfred Galbraith, the editor of the *Anniston Star*. Being the only newspaper in Anniston, the *Star* had a great deal of influence, from an informational as well as editorial viewpoint. While the *Star* gave much objective coverage to the events that happened, it appeared to use judgment in trying not to report in such a way as to create and inflame crises. Its editorials tried to be fair and called for the solving of racial problems through communication and negotiation.

There is little doubt that Wilfred felt real tension between his role as editor of the free press newspaper, whose job was to keep the community informed of issues and situations that affected the community, and his being a member of the Council. The nature of what was happening and the ever-present possibility of violence required that much of the Council's work be behind the scenes activity which would serve the community best if it were not publicized in the newspaper. Wilfred basically respected the need for careful discrimination of what should be reported about the Council's work. I think he felt as journalists do in times of war or other extreme crisis when the press to some extent censors itself for the good of the country or the community. There's no doubt that we were locally engaged in a sort of war.

The fact that Anniston was a relatively small city (about thirty-five thousand population) made it possible for people to know each other. For instance, before the appointment of the Human Relations Committee, I knew fairly well all but one of the white members, and I knew very well two of the black members. In the Council's early meetings, we tried to have the Council members develop good personal relationships and to conduct themselves in such a way that both respect and trust could develop. For the most part, this approach worked and added to the ability of the Council to do its work in a united way. To my amazement, nearly every vote we took in the Council in the early days was unanimous!

In addition to the original members of the Human Relations Council, many others played important parts. One such person was George Smitherman, the minister of Mount Calvary Baptist Church. He was appointed later to the Council. He worked along with Nimrod and Bob to represent the particular issues and interests of Anniston's black community. I don't mean to imply by that statement that they represented only the black interests; one of the accomplishments of the Council was that the white members and the black members were coming together to bring progress to the entire Anniston community, which is a way of saying we were engaged in an experiment to see if we could nurture into existence true democracy.

George Smitherman became a special friend of mine. He always wore sharp pointed black shoes and a narrow necktie. I always wondered where he got the shoes! He would come often out to my office at the First Presbyterian Church, just to talk. He would tell me what was happening in the black community and I would share with him what I saw happening in the white community. It was a good and healthy source of communication. Among the black Baptist churches, the Seventeenth Street Baptist Church, of which Nimrod was minister, was composed of the more educated and leading citizens of the black community. George's church, Mount Calvary Baptist Church, had many more members who were not as well educated and some who could not read or write. I always thought this was why George was so quick to express himself in language that was clear and graphic. He could always tell a story that almost perfectly fit a given situation. There were two occasions when his comments were vivid illustrations of this. Perhaps one reason I appreciated them is that they are comments that have a rural setting, and being from a farm in Mississippi, I could relate to them.

In 1966 two members of the congregation of First Presbyterian Church did a very generous thing for me. They paid for me to go to New College in Edinburgh, Scotland, for what was called the "Summer Term," in April and May. When I got to Scotland in early April, I nearly froze to death as I began the "Summer" term! The two members arranged for my wife Betty to come to Edinburgh at the end of the term, and then for us to take the "Grand Tour" of Europe. I think our generous friends, the Jespersons and Turners, realized it would be better for the church if their minister had a bit more education!

On one occasion when George came to my office I told him of my plans. I probably went into great detail and embellished the trip considerably knowing it would really get his attention. When I finished my elaborate description of what Mrs. Noble and I were going to do, and some of the major historical things we were going to see, George said,

"Great God, Brother Noble!" (He always called me Brother Noble.) Then he said, "When I was a little boy on the farm in North Carolina, my father would take corn to the grist mill to be ground. I would often go along with him. I would stand around and watch the corn being ground. Of course, the air was filled with the meal dust and the men grinding the corn would be covered with the dust. Before long the meal dust would be all over me too. It would be on my clothes, in my hair and even in my eyebrows and eyelashes. You couldn't tell me from the men working there. Now, when you come back, Brother Noble, I want to come out here and let you tell me all about what you have seen and done. I want to let it 'get all over me' so folks can't tell whether I have been there or not."

The other occasion was when he asked to say a special word to the Ministerial Association. The white and black associations by this time had been merged into one organization. At this particular meeting we were gathered at the First Methodist Church in one of their Sunday School rooms. There were rows of chairs facing a lectern at the front of the room. At the end of the meeting, George, from the back of the room said, "Mr. President, are we finished with the meeting?" The president replied that we were finished. Then George said, "May I say a word to the group?"

The situation was that George had gotten into trouble with his church and also had some family problems. As was often the case, when someone active in civil rights "got into trouble," it would be news. So the local paper had carried an article about the problems of Rev. Smitherman, and had included a picture of him in the paper. Every minister in the room knew he had "gotten into trouble."

So George walked to the front of the room and stood behind the lectern. This is what he said: "Brethren, when I was a little boy on the farm in North Carolina, one day I carried a bucket of slop to the pig lot back of the house. I set the bucket down to unlock the gate to the pigpen. There was a mother hen with her biddies there that started picking at the slop bucket. One of the little biddies fell into the slop bucket. I got him out, but he was covered with the slop. Now, that mother hen and all the other little biddies would have nothing to do with the little biddy that had fallen into the slop. [Then George paused a few beats.] Now brethren, I have fallen into a bucket of slop, and I don't want you all to stop having anything to do with me." It was a perfect analogy, and most of us did not desert our friend because he had gotten into trouble.

Some years later when I was minister of First (Scots) Presbyterian Church in Charleston, South Carolina, George called me several times. It was usually when something was happening in Anniston relating to race. At one point his church was going to honor him for his years of service. He asked me to come and be the principal speaker. I regret that I was not able to accept his invitation, but I will always be grateful that I got to know him and could become his friend.

The fact that the Anniston Ministerial Association had had Union Holy Week services for years created a good pattern for worship across denominational lines. When the white and black Ministerial Associations merged, it became possible for the Holy Week services to be open to all races. Even though at the beginning the services were held in City Hall (public property), they were a symbol of unity between the black and white religious leaders in the community.

While there was a White Citizen's Council in Anniston, it did not appear to be large or broad in its outreach among white citizens. It may have been that the KKK was already quite strong in the Anniston area and therefore the White Citizen's Council was redundant. However, the general segregationist attitude throughout the white community did make the Human Relations Council's work more difficult. There were wonderful exceptions to this, but many people who would not join a White Citizen's Council or the KKK nonetheless quietly favored the mission if not the methods of these white supremacist organizations.

In my own case, the members of First Presbyterian Church did not outwardly oppose my work, nor did they vigorously support it. By and large, they silently watched. Privately, some gave me moral support. The attitude in the congregation ranged from some strong support to the extreme attitude expressed by an elder. His comment which came at the time of the assassination of Martin Luther King, Jr., was some three years after I had resigned from the Human Relations Council, but it revealed an extreme racist attitude. "I'm glad," he told me, "King got just what he deserved." Then, knowing my attitude, he slunk away as I looked at him with pity.

Such an attitude in one who was a Presbyterian elder and a respected citizen in the community, and the fact that he was not alone in his viewpoint, as well as the strong desire in the black community to remove the patterns of segregation as soon as possible, made it necessary to maintain a delicate balance if violence was to be avoided. One of the reasons for the success we had was that we were able for the most part to maintain that balance. We made enough progress so that the black community did not feel completely frustrated, and at the same time, the progress was gradual enough so that the white community accepted it.

The publishing of the "Anniston Manifesto" revealed how anxious the black community was for more rapid progress. But while it was a strong stimulus to move more quickly, the pattern of negotiation had been established and ultimately prevailed. This is not to say that there were not serious struggles yet to come. There were numerous problems to be dealt with and many would cause much tension in the community. However, in spite of the anxiety and tensions, the precedent to solve problems through communication, negotiation, and mutual respect continued until the mid-1980s and perhaps even to the present time. In the winter 2000 issue of the Southern Poverty Law Center's *Intelligence Report,* there is a listing of the "Active Hate Groups in the U.S. in 1999." Considering the past history of the Ku Klux Klan and some other groups in Anniston it was wonderfully surprising to find no hate group listed in Anniston! There was not even a web-site promoting such hate groups! I hope it is still true today as it was in 1999.[53]

Interestingly, there was never any public expression of appreciation for the original nine members of the Council or for me as its first chairman. That, too, was a part of the scene where if too much had been made of it, it might have created a backlash. However, when I left Anniston in 1971, six years after being on the Human Relations Council, the Anniston City Council (the form of government had changed from a commission to a council), passed a special resolution. The resolution was drawn up by Dr. Gordon A. Rodgers, a black dentist who was the first black person ever to sit on the city's governing body. His election in itself shows the change that had occurred in Anniston. The resolution read:

> All too seldom there comes to a community a man who in truth is a "man for all seasons." A man who serves the community in troubled times and in times secure. A man who was so often the bridge over troubled waters. A man who had the great faculty for bringing out the best in all of us. A man whose dedication to God and his fellow man knew no limits—even when faced with great personal tragedy*. Such a man is the Reverend J. Phillips Noble. On behalf of a grateful city, we, the Anniston City Council, extend to him our sincerest thanks—and we wish him Godspeed in all his future endeavors.
>
> PASSED AND ADOPTED this 20th day of July, 1971.[54]

The fact that this resolution was introduced by the only black member of the Council meant that it expressed the larger appreciation from the black community that I had tried to help in bringing about change through the Human Relations Council. Though that appreciation was never made public, it was and continues to be meaningful to me that the community, and especially the black community, made an expression of appreciation.

To say the least, this was an interesting and challenging decade in our nation and in Anniston, Alabama. Even though it was a difficult time, Anniston found a way through it with a measure of peace, and what is more, it brought freedom, justice, and opportunity to so many who had been denied it for so long.

The patterns of segregation that had dehumanized a whole race of people were changed. A social revolution had occurred in Anniston!

*A reference to the death of our thirteen-year-old son, Scott, who died of leukemia in 1968.

Thirty Years Later

T HE SUN PEEKED OVER Tenth Street Mountain and cast its early light on the town of Anniston. A few tall buildings reflected the first rays of the sun and here and there a church steeple pointed to the clear sky.

> For Lo, the winter is past,
> The rain is over and gone;
> The flowers appear on the earth;
> The time of the singing of birds is come,
> And the voice of the turtle-dove is heard in our land.[55]

What a marvelous spring weekend it was to be visiting in Anniston. I had said to my wife, Betty, "It has been a long time since our whole family has been to Anniston. Let's get Betty [our daughter] and Phil [our son] and go spend Mother's Day weekend there. We can see some old friends and reminisce about our years there."

Betty said, "If we are going to spend Saturday night there, we should make motel reservations."

I said, "I don't think that is necessary. Anniston is not crowded. We can get rooms at the Holiday Inn."

So here we were, the four of us, in a car pulling off Interstate 20 to go into Anniston. The Holiday Inn was on the right, and we pulled in to get

Betty and Phil Noble 2000.

two rooms for Saturday night. When I went to the desk to ask for rooms, the receptionist, an attractive black woman, said, "Let me look. I am not sure I have two rooms available." While she looked at her records, I noticed several young black men and women in the lobby. The receptionist said to me, "I did not know whether or not we had rooms available, because this is spring break for Auburn University and the University of Alabama and the black college students are having a conference here. But I find we do have two non-smoking rooms available."

As it was about noon, we stopped at a restaurant for a bite of lunch. We recognized a man who had been a member of First Presbyterian Church when I was pastor there, but I could not recall his name. He was sitting at the table with a black man. I wondered if that good Presbyterian had taken the black man to lunch, or if the black man had taken him!

After lunch we walked along Noble Street and tried to recall just what stores had existed when we were here. There was Belk's. When we stepped inside, a nicely dressed young black man said, "Welcome to Belk's. May I help you?" We really didn't want anything. We were just looking around. There had been a couple of banks on Noble Street when we lived here, so we looked in one to see what changes had been made in the modernized lobby. There were a few people standing in line at the three cashiers' windows. Two of the cashiers were black and one was white. As we came out of the bank, two policemen were strolling down the street. One was white and one was black.

We called a few friends and visited in the afternoon with a couple of the older ones. On the way we passed by the municipal golf course. When I glimpsed two white and two black men, I instinctively thought, my mind wandering in thirty-year memories, "I didn't know they still had caddies here," but then I realized it was just four friends playing golf.

Dinner that night was in the nicest restaurant in Anniston, and we could not help noticing that at several tables black couples were having a quiet dinner.

The next day, Mother's Day, we went to church at the First Presbyterian Church. It was a wonderful and warm experience for the four of us as we saw many friends who were there during the fifteen years when I was the minister. The sanctuary was as beautiful as ever. The magnificent stained glass window over the chancel was still brilliant. The window with the symbol of the crown representing "the King of Kings, and Lord of Lords" had been put in the very day that John F. Kennedy was killed. We read in the bulletin that the churches of Anniston would be celebrating Unity Sunday the next week. Pulpits were going to be exchanged across denominational and racial lines.

It being Mother's Day, we took a flowering plant and put it on our son

Scott's grave at the cemetery. As we drove through the cemetery, we saw the headstones of many people who had died since we had lived here.

A new library had been built since we were here, and we wanted to see it. On the way, we had to pull over to let a fire engine with its siren blaring get by. We couldn't help noticing that of the four firemen on the truck, one was black.

When we got to the library on Mother's Day afternoon, there were women and children and a few men around on the grounds. We went in to the receptionist desk and indicated that we had lived here a number of years ago and we would like to find some information that might be in the old files. The receptionist said, "Glena, the reference librarian will help you. She is at the desk in the room to the right." When we went to her desk, we were warmly met by a smartly dressed young black woman who seemed glad to help us. It was so quiet and peaceful in and around the library with families and children coming and going. It made us want to stay.

We could not stay, however, because even though we had arranged a late check-out time, we had to go if we were going to have time for a bit of lunch before we checked out. As we went into one of the hamburger chains, we saw a black man and his little four-year-old son coming out, and the father was saying, "Hold your hamburger tight, son, so you won't drop it."

We checked out of the Holiday Inn and noticed that many of the black students were also leaving. It had been a quiet, peaceful and loving Mother's Day. As the sun began to set across the ridge of mountains on the west side of Anniston and as we turned east on I-20 headed back to Atlanta, I said to my children, "Phil, we did not do everything. There is still plenty for you and Betty and your friends to do. But we did do some things! Thanks be to God."

Appendix

A. Where they are now . . .

ORIGINAL HRC MEMBERS

Raleigh Byrd is retired in Chicago, Illinois.

Edwin Cosper died in 1997.

Wilfred Galbraith died in 1988.

Marcus A. Howze died in 1991.

William B. McClain is professor of preaching and worship at Wesley Theological Seminary, Washington, D.C.

Grant Oden died in 1981.

Nimrod Quintus Reynolds remains pastor of Anniston's Seventeenth Street Baptist Church; president of the local chapter of SCLC; and secretary of the national SCLC Board.

Leonard Roberts died in 1985.

J. Phillips Noble is retired in Decatur, Georgia, and serves as pastor to pastors in the Greater Atlanta Presbytery.

OTHER INDIVIDUALS WHO PLAYED MAJOR ROLES

Mayor Claude Dear is retired in Anniston.

Miller Sproull is retired in Anniston.

Jack Suggs is deceased.

Charles Doster practices law in Anniston.

Kenneth Adams died in 1989.

Charles Keyes is deceased.

J. B. Stoner served a prison sentence for bombing a black church and is now deceased.

Brandt Ayers is publisher of the *Anniston Star*.

Edward Wood is retired in Anniston.

George Smitherman is deceased.

B. "R. Kennedy, Others, 'Hanged' at Rally"

(This Anniston Star *article was accompanied by a photograph of hanged effigies of James Farmer, chairman of the Congress of Racial Equality (CORE), which had sponsored the Freedom Rides; U.S. Attorney General Robert Kennedy; Anniston-based FBI agents Clay Slate and Joe Landers; and FBI Director J. Edgar Hoover.)*

The United States Attorney General, three members of the Federal Bureau of Investigation and a member of the Congress of Racial Equality were hanged in effigy at a rally staged on West 10th Street Tuesday night. Vick Ashurst of Montgomery said the rally was sponsored by the National States' Rights Party, of which he is state president. He said the group was organizing an Anniston unit, and had held several meetings in the area weekly. The rally was held on a lot in front of a welder's shop, and Kenneth Adams, local Ku Klux Klan leader, said the property had been leased for the purpose. An initial crowd estimated at 200 gathered on the scene as a scaffolding with dangling nooses was set up and the dummies with placards across their fronts were hoisted into the air. Many left, however, when a shower sprinkled the area as a man who identified himself as J. B. Stoner, Atlanta attorney for the organization, launched into an attack on the FBI, the policies of the federal government, the attorney general, CORE, the NAACP, the Mayor of Atlanta, the head of the Atlanta School Board, 'many Southern newspapers,' and others. Stoner bitterly criticized the indictment by a federal grand jury of Kenneth Adams and eight other Annistonians in connection with the burning here several weeks ago of a Greyhound bus. He described the indictments as a 'Communist conspiracy,' and charged that 'Freedom Riders' on the bus had started the fire themselves. Speaking over a public address system arranged atop a flatbed truck, Stoner urged his listeners to join the States' Righters, which lists among its aims 'the creation of a wholesome White Folk Community' throughout the South and the nation."

C. Anniston Manifesto *(Excerpted)*

The text of the Constitution of the United States of America or the Preamble says: 'We, the people of the United States, in order to form a more perfect union, establish justice, insure domestic tranquility, provide for the common defense, promote the general welfare, and secure the blessings of liberty, to ourselves and our posterity, do ordain and establish this Constitution for the United States of America.'

This text, or the essence thereof has been on the desk of every school teacher, been recited by almost every student, written into the thesis of many college professors. This text refers to 'We the people.'

May we make it crystal clear in Anniston, Alabama, 'The Model City,' it is 'We the people.' By this we mean Negro people. We are the last hired, the first fired, the one discriminated against and the one of the lowest income bracket. Referring to the text again 'to establish justice,' how just is justice? Anniston, our 'Model City,' with a multi-million dollar business to serve and to share her profits with her fair sons and daughters, for a hundred years has mistreated part of her children.

The Negroes, whose blood and strength felled her trees, dug her foundation with their own strength, have enjoyed the least of her blessings. The Negro has been patient but in her patience her dreams have been smashed, her hopes have died. The City Government, whose livelihood began not by the ingenuity but on the strength of Negro blood, sacrifice, sweat and tears. You said long ago that the Negro needed an education, he needed to clean-up. Even though you shut him out of your schools he sought to qualify himself in schools out of your city and out of our state. Even with the Ph.D., you ignore him, even with skilled labor you give him him the lowest positions.

We asked you several times to give us a position on your boards, but you have denied us our request. We have taken your humiliation and abuse without the slightest degree of retaliation. But you have distorted our faith in your word justice. You have betrayed our trust, you have wounded our dignity. Our City Fathers have said that they wanted peace. They did not want demonstrations, they did not want 'outside agitators,' but at the same time they have refused to hire blacks as secretaries, clerks, managers, policemen, firemen and filling any other position. Are demonstrations, protests, pickets, etc., the only way the Negro can be integrated into the huge business of our city? Has his labor been in vain? Has his patience been abused? Has the color of his skin made you hate him and discriminate against him? God forbid! It has been said that 'It is better to die in the streets than to die on your knees.'

We have been on our knees for one hundred years, yea, nearly 350 years. We want equal representation in jobs and accommodations, and we want it now. We want Negroes on our city boards and we want it now. We want the veil of segregation and discrimination lifted and we want it lifted now. We want the Negro employees of our city upgraded and we want it now. We want Negro firemen and we want them now. We want to have the freedom to go to any city park and swimming pool and we want that freedom now. How long is long enough? Is 100 years long enough to wait? Will we have to wait another year, yea, another 100 years for first class citizenship, for freedom? We want our freedom and we want it now. We want the black sons and daughters of Anniston emancipated and we want them emancipated now. If you will not plunge into the battle of war against poverty then we have no other alternative than to wage that battle alone. If you must continue to breed pools of poverty among the Negroes of this city by failing to hire the Negro in proportion to whites, and by failing to give social security and insurance against casualties and disabilities, then we have no other alternative than to rise up in protest to the abuses and injustices we have suffered so long. How long is long enough, rather, how long is too long?

We are all of the same blood? We would like to know why it is that in the offices of the professional men of our city, especially the doctors, Negroes are herded up like cattle in a small box like room sweating it out until they are called, and yet the white patients may relax in comfort until they are called. In many instances, Negroes, even with an appointment must wait until all of the white patients have been seen before they can be waited on. Isn't our money the same as the white man's? Can't we be served on an equal basis and not be treated like 'seconds'? When one's health and even his life is at stake, can we be shoved aside? There are approximately 30,000 telephones in this district comprising Anniston, Oxford, Hobson City, Ohatchee, and Eastaboga. According to the population of white and Negro subscribers, the Negro subscribers are about 25 percent less. The Negro subscribers pay their bills or else their service is discontinued. New lines are built, new facilities are installed, new jobs are given but not to 'We the people.' A survey was made a few years ago, and it was noted that here in the state of Alabama there are more Negro school teachers employed in both city and county systems with more degrees, than white.

Why can't some of our very fine teachers become telephone operators, clerks and cashiers? Why can't some of our college professors become managers? If the telephone company is to serve 'We the people,' and 'We the people' pay the bills and there is to be justice, why is it that the Negro does not share in the jobs and training programs of this ever expanding industry? The text also states 'To insure domestic tranquility.' Has the Negro's livelihood been overlooked as domestic? How just is it for the electric utility company to sell its power to 'We the people' and 'We the people' pay our bills, and many of these bills are paid by people here in Anniston who earn less than fifteen dollars a week, but these are Negro people. Expansions are made by the profits made by this huge business but when it comes to good jobs that pay well, they are not for the Negro. The local gas company is another public facility. It serves all the people. 'We the people' pay our share but who is he that reads the meters? Who maintains the facilities? Who drives all of the trucks? Who is employed in the various offices? It is not 'We the people.' Where is justice? Where is domestic tranquility? Article XIV of the text states: 'All persons born or naturalized in the United States, and subject to the jurisdiction thereof, are citizens of the United States and of the state wherein they reside.'

We the Negro people in Anniston are citizens of the United States residing in the state of Alabama, why then can't we share in jobs and job opportunities the same as the white citizens? We take pride in the fact that we are living in the 'Land of the free and the home of the brave,' but how free and brave is America? One of the basic reasons that the pilgrims left England and came to America was freedom of religion. This rich religious heritage has been handed to us from past generations, but not without tarnish. Ironically, one of the most segregated institutions in America is the Church. It teaches God's love for all men but does not live in its teachings. Negroes have been turned away and asked to leave the House of God in many places across our democratic country. One cannot believe that this is the true Christian religion in action. The Church should represent the total truth of God.

A Church that segregates says that God is a lie and He does not love all men, only some men; a church that closes its doors to a group of people because of their race is turning back the clock of destiny to sacrilegious heathenism. It is a perversion of the church's purpose and a distortion of its sacred ideals. This is bigotry and hypocrisy at the most. This is a mockery of God. Why can't all churches of Anniston open their doors to all people? John Oxenham so graphically stated, 'In Christ there is no East or West, in Him no South or North; But one great fellowship of love throughout the whole wide earth.' Amendment XV of the Constitution of the United States says: 'The right of citizens of the United States to vote shall not be denied or abridged by the United States or any state on account of race, color or previous conditions of servitude.'

But here in the Calhoun County Court House the rights of Negroes to register to vote is flagrantly violated. White people are registered as fast as they present themselves to the Board, while Negroes are restricted to two and sometimes three applicants being processed at one time, even though they are the only persons to be registered. This slow down technique causes Negro applicants to accumulate in a long waiting line. It certainly abridges their constitutional rights to the ballot and is humiliating.

When a citizen has been taught from childhood to sing America, My Country 'Tis of Thee, Sweet Land of Liberty, Of Thee I Sing, and truly it is my country, America. Instead of from every Mountainside Let Freedom Ring, it is from the Highways of our country we listen to hear shotguns blast our heads from our bodies. Highpower rifle bullets wounding us mortally in our backs. Our children massacred in our churches, from blasts of dynamite, our churches burned in ashes, our Negro ministers beaten with pipes, chains, and stabbed with knives and even men have been castrated, not to let freedom ring, but to keep freedom from ringing. The third stanza of America says in part 'Let mortal tongues awake, Let all that breathe partake, Let rocks their silence break, the sound prolong.' The Negroes of Anniston think it is time for every mortal tongue of the Ministry, every tongue of the entire Christian World, even the rocks in the mountains should cry That God hath made of one blood, All Nations of Men, for to dwell on all the face of the earth— If it is My Country, 'tis of thee, Why can't we share in its benefits, Our Model City 'And Judgment is turned away backward, and justice standeth afar off: For truth is fallen in the streets; and equity cannot enter.' Isa. 59:14"

D. "Reply to Anniston Manifesto," September 19, 1964, issue of "The Keyes Report"

"When Karl Marx wrote the Communist Manifesto in 1847 setting forth the principles of Communism, few people of that day ever thought it would amount to anything. Marx died with very few followers. However, his Manifesto was the seed well planted and, only 70 years later, after the Russian Revolution of 1917, Nickolai Lenin used the principles of the Communist Manifesto to set up the first Socialist Government.

Communism grew under Stalin, and now under Krushchev, to the point that, in only 47 years after the revolution, the Communists control two thirds of the land area of the world and over one third of the world's population. In comparison it took over 1900 years for Christianity to reach a world population of 916 million people; whereas, it took only 47 years for the Communists, using the principle of the Godless Communism of the Marx Manifesto, to reach a world population of over one billion people. The total world population at present is 3 billion 150 million.

Why was this allowed to happen? Because of the apathy of the people and because they keep swallowing the controlled propaganda put out by the press, radio and television that 'it can't happen.' But it keeps on happening and expanding all over the world. Now, you might wonder why I wrote the above message. In the Anniston Star of Sunday, September 13, 1964, page 7A, there appeared another Manifesto. This one was called the Anniston Manifesto. If you haven't read it, I advise you to do so, and to read it carefully. It could very well have been called the Negro Manifesto as it sets forth their intentions, motives, or principles of action. First, I would like to call to your attention that N. Q. Reynolds is President, G. E. Smitherman Vice President and Grant Oden, Treasurer of the Calhoun County Improvement Association. Their names appear on the Manifesto. They are also the colored members of the Bi-Racial Committee which is now known as the Human Relations Counsel which consists of nine members including five white citizens and four colored citizens.

This committee was appointed by the Anniston City Commission with the apparent idea of integrating the colored race with the white race at such a pace that the white people would not notice it until they woke up and found themselves completely integrated. Few people realize how much integration has taken place since the formation of the bi-racial committee because it hasn't been publicized. But, so far, the water fountains and rest rooms of many businesses have been integrated, next the library, the variety store lunch counters, the municipal golf course, the theatres and some of the restaurants, and some colored people have attended many of the heretofore white churches.

But Messrs. Reynolds, Smitherman, and Oden, officers and leaders of the Negro organization that sponsored the Manifesto which indicated that they are dissatisfied with the progress made by the bi-racial committee, of which they are members, so far as I can learn, did not show a copy of the Manifesto to the white members of the bi-racial committee before it was printed. By their actions they have demonstrated that there is no need for a bi-racial committee in Anniston. They have indicated in the Manifesto that it is better to die in the street than to wait any longer for total integration which they are demanding.

In talking with N. Q. Reynolds on the phone, he said to me that the Manifesto wasn't written to appease the white people, but that the Manifesto expressed their demands. Also, if we didn't meet certain demands, that they had no alternative than to wage the battle alone. That might be a very good experience for them as they would soon find out how far they have advanced in the past 100 years since slavery with the help of the white man. They seem to have plenty of radios, automobiles, telephones and a great many live in nice government project homes gas heated and lighted by electricity and financed by the taxes paid by the white man.

If they don't believe they have advanced under this system, let them take a trip to the African Congo and see if their colored cousins have all the above-mentioned luxuries. This country is 90 percent white and only 10 percent Negro and yet all that one hears and reads about is the economic plight of the Negro when there are just as many white people who are out of work and are hard-pressed economically. But we do not read of them rioting in the streets, hurting innocent people, attacking police, destroying private property and looting stores as happened in New York, Brooklyn, Philadelphia, Rochester and many other cities in the United States. A kindly word of warning to the Negro race which represents only 10 percent of the population of the U.S. One of these days you will push the white people just a little bit too hard and you will wake up wishing you had never heard of Martin Luther King, leaders of CORE and NAACP who will lead you down the road to destruction. To the white readers: If the Anniston Manifesto has the same success as the Communist Manifesto, not you, but your children and grandchildren, will be the victims. The Manifesto stated that 'We are all the same blood.' But God never meant for it to be mixed because, when you do, you get neither pure Negro nor pure white, but a mixed mongrel offspring."

E. "The Willie Brewster Murder"

(from *Free At Last, a History of the Civil Rights Movement and Those who Died in the Struggle*)

On the night of July 15, 1965, about 100 white people gathered at the courthouse in Anniston, Alabama, to hear Connie Lynch speak. He told the audience there should be a special medal for whoever killed Viola Liuzzo. He promised that all politicians who supported civil rights efforts would be hanged when the National States Rights Party took over the country. He went on to say, "If it takes killing to get the Negroes out of the white man's streets and to protect our constitutional rights, then I say yes, kill them."

Sitting at the podium while Lynch spoke as J. B. Stoner, the NSRP lawyer who made a business of defending Klansmen and others charged with racist crimes. Next to Stoner was Kenneth Adams, another NSRP official who owned part of a local oil distribution business, and who once assaulted the famous black singer Nat King Cole at a concert in Birmingham. In the audience was one of Adams' employees, 23-year-old Hubert Damon Strange, and his friend, Jimmy Knight. About the time Lynch's tirade reached its peak, three black men were getting off work from a local pipe foundry. One of them was Willie Brewster, a hard-working 38-year-old who raised his own vegetable garden in addition to working at the factory.

When the shift ended on the night of July 15, Brewster got in a co-worker's car for the ride home to Munford, a small town 20 miles from Anniston, where Brewster's pregnant wife, Lestine, was waiting with their two small children.

Willie Brewster was described by his boss as someone who 'went beyond his duties to help.' When his friend complained of aching feet during the drive home, Brewster took over the wheel. He was driving down Highway 202 when three gunshot blasts tore through the back window.

A bullet slammed into Brewster's spine and he slumped over the wheel. The uninjured riders caught a glimpse of several white men in a passing car as they tried to regain control of their own vehicle. For the next several days, Lestine Brewster sat with her husband at the hospital while a local newspaper raised reward money for information leading to his assailants. The reward offer, wrote an Anniston Star editor, 'says to Willie Brewster and to the world that he is not alone at this moment, that the persons who brought him to the point of death...are not just his enemies. They are enemies of us all, and we stand together in opposition to them.' Civic leaders raised $20,000 within 12 hours and Alabama Governor George Wallace added another $1,000 to the reward fund.

The doctors told Lestine that if her husband lived, he would be paralyzed from the waist down. Willie tried to reassure his wife, saying, 'I'm going to get well.' But three days after the shooting, he died. Lestine had to be hospitalized immediately, and a month later she lost her baby through miscarriage. Three white men—Hubert Damon Strange, Johnny Ira Defries and Lewis Blevins— were indicted for the murder of Willie Brewster on August 27, 1965. Strange, the first to be tried, was represented by NSRP (National States Rights Party) lawyer J. B. Stoner. Jimmy Knight, who had attended the NSRP meeting with Strange, was the star prosecution witness. He testified that he heard Strange boast, 'we got us a nigger' after the shooting.

After 13 hours of deliberation and 20 ballots, the all-white jury returned a second-degree murder conviction against Strange and sentenced him to 10 years in prison. It was the first time during the civil rights era that a white person was convicted of killing a black person in Alabama. The guilty verdict astonished everyone, including civil rights leaders who had already made plans to protest an acquittal. Hubert Strange never served his prison term. While he was free on bond awaiting appeal, he got into a barroom brawl with another man and was killed. Johnny Ira Defries was acquitted of murder in a second trial. In 1980 Stoner himself was convicted for the racial bombing of a church in Birmingham. He was released from prison in 1986 after serving several years, and returned to his white supremacist activities.

F. Phil Noble to Claude Dear, April 29, 1965

Dear Mayor Dear:

For the past two years I have served on Anniston's Human Relations Council by your appointment. For the first year and one-half I was Chairman. I am grateful to you for giving me this opportunity to serve my community. As you well know, when this council began its work, none of us knew what the outcome would be. Each of us did suspect that there would be harsh criticisms, misunderstandings, added difficulties in our chosen fields of work, certain harassments for ourselves and our families, and even threats of physical violence and other intimidations.

What we suspected along these lines has happened. However, we believe many good results have attended our work—results which at the beginning we hoped for, but without any assurance that they would come. Without attempting to detail any of these good results, I simply point to the fact that during the last two years cities and communities all about us have had untold racial problems dealt with at the conference table. It is my hope that a pattern has been set in dealing with our problems which will increasingly result in community good will, fairness, and wholeness. Since I have now served for two years, and since it is our opinion that some new members should be appointed each year, thereby broadening the base of support for the council and also distributing the responsibility for its work; therefore, I shall not accept further appointment to the Human Relations Council upon the expiration of this year's term.

I have indicated above some of the difficulties we have encountered for the past two years to assure you that it is not because of these or fear of them that I ask to be replaced on the council. If this were the case I would not have agreed to serve at the beginning and certainly would not have continued for two years. I have also pointed out something of the past success of our work to indicate that it is my belief that the council is in a good strong position to continue to work effectively in the future and that it can do so better with some new personnel. In my asking to be replaced on the council, please be assured that I shall be no less interested in the welfare of our whole community and all its people, and I will continue to seek to render what service I can in its behalf.

Sincerely yours,

J. Phillips Noble

NOTES

Notes to the Introduction

1. Daniel Letwin, *The Challenge of Interracial Unionism: Alabama Coal Miners, 1878-1921* (Chapel Hill:University of North Carolina Press, 1998)

2. Dan T. Carter, *The Politics of Rage: George Wallace, The Origins of the New Conservatism, and the Transformation of American Politics* (New York: Simon and Schuster, 1995), p. 27, and Glenn T. Eskew, *But for Birmingham: The Local and National Movements in the Civil Rights Struggle* (Chapel Hill: University of North Carolina Press, 1997), pp. 114-118.

3. Eskew, p. 138

4. Eskew, p. 138.

5. Eskew, pp. 113-114.

Notes to the Main Text

1. *Eyes on the Prize,* Juan Williams, p. 148.

2. *Free at Last, a History of the Civil Rights Movement and Those who Died in the Struggle,* p. 20-21.

3. Letter from Dr. William B. McClain undated, but around March 18, 1991.

4. *The Greatest Generation,* Tom Brokaw, p. 195.

5. Ibid., p. 196, 198.

6. Ibid., p. 199-200

7. Ibid., p. 200.

8. *Civil Rights and Wrongs,* Harry S. Ashmore, p. xiv

9. *Unlikely Heroes,* Jack Bass, p. 328.

10. Ibid., p. 310.

11. Ibid., p. 328.

12. *Civil Rights and Wrongs,* Harry S. Ashmore, p. 112.

13. *Eyes on the Prize,* Juan Williams, p. 39.

14. *Free at Last, a History of the Civil Rights Movement and Those who Died in the Struggle,* p. 40-41.

15. *Unlikely Heroes,* Jack Bass, p. 152.

16. Taped interview with Messrs. Reynolds, Wood, Grier, Tolbert and Stringer, March 11, 1991.

17. Ibid.

18. Ibid.

19. From Mayor Claude Dear's scrapbook.

20. *Anniston Star,* November 13, 1962.

21. Ibid., February 22, 1963.

22. From the John F. Kennedy Library, Harvard University.

23. *Anniston Star,* May 13, 1963.

24. Minutes of the City Commission, Anniston, Alabama.

25. Ibid.

26. *Anniston Star,* May 17, 1963.

27. Ibid., May 20, 1963.

28. Ibid.

29. Ibid.

30. Interview with Mayor Claude Dear.

31. *Anniston Star,* May 27, 1963.

32. Ibid.

33. Ibid.

34. *Free at Last, a History of the Civil Rights Movement and Those who Died in the Struggle,* p. 80.

35. Taped interview with Messrs. Reynolds, Wood, Grier, Tolbert and Stringer, March 11, 1991.

36. Sermon: "Having Church at Sweethome, Alabama: The Journey of an Alabama Preacher Boy" by William B. McClain.

37. *Anniston Star,* Monday, September 16, 1963.

38. Minutes of the Session, First Presbyterian Church, Anniston, Alabama, October 27, 1963.

39. From the John F. Kennedy Library, Harvard University.

40. The Anniston Star, November 13, 1963.

41. Taped interview with Messrs. Reynolds, Wood, Grier, Tolbert and Stringer, March 11, 1991.

42. Interview with Mayor Claude Dear.

43. *Free at Last, a History of the Civil Rights Movement and Those who Died in the Struggle,* p. 59.

44. Ibid., p. 80.

45. From Complaint Report: Investigative and Identification Division, Department of Public Safety.

46. Telephone conversation with Robert Field, Anniston attorney.

47. Correspondence with Brandt Ayers, Publisher of the *Anniston Star,* Anniston, Alabama.

48. Ibid.

49. Ibid.

50. Ibid.

51. Letter from J. Phillips Noble files.

52. Aaron Henry, *The Fire Ever Burning,* by Constance Curry, University Press of Mississippi, 2000, p. 146.

53. Southern Poverty Law Center's *Intelligence Report,* Winter 2000, Issue 97.

54. Minutes of the Anniston City Council, July 20, 1971.

55. The Bible, Song of Solomon 2:11-12.

Index

In 1963, the Rev. Nimrod Q. Reynolds, right above, was attacked by white supremacists as he and the Rev. William B. McClain (not pictured) attempted to desegregate the Anniston Public Library. Forty years later, Rev. Reynolds stood outside the Liles Memorial Anniston Public Library with Harry R. Malone, the 2003 chairman of the Library Board of Anniston and Calhoun County.